Bound to Last

BOUND TO LAST

30 Writers on Their Most Cherished Book

EDITED BY

Sean Manning

FOREWORD BY

Ray Bradbury

Da Capo Press
A Member of the Perseus Books Group

Designed by Brent Wilcox
Set in 11.25 point Minion Pro by the Perseus Books Group

Library of Congress Cataloging-in-Publication Data
Bound to last : 30 writers on their most cherished book /
edited by Sean Manning ; foreword by Ray Bradbury.
    p.   cm.
ISBN 978-0-306-81921-6 (pbk. : alk. paper)
    1. Authors, American—Books and reading.   2. Authors—
Books and reading.   I. Manning, Sean.
Z1039.A87B68 2010
028'.9—dc22
                                                2010026247

Published by Da Capo Press
A Member of the Perseus Books Group
www.dacapopress.com

Da Capo Press books are available at special discounts for bulk
purchases in the U.S. by corporations, institutions, and other
organizations. For more information, please contact the Special
Markets Department at the Perseus Books Group,
2300 Chestnut Street, Suite 200, Philadelphia, PA 19103,
or call (800) 810-4145, ext. 5000, or e-mail
special.markets@perseusbooks.com.

10 9 8 7 6 5 4 3 2 1

CONTENTS

Contents

Contents

FOREWORD

Ray Bradbury

When I was nine years old I had my wonderful Aunt Neva living above me in our house in Waukegan, Illinois. She was my constant companion. Being only eleven years older than myself, she was more a sister than an aunt. She surrounded me with books and miniature theaters that she built and paintings that she painted. Neva allowed me to prowl around her studio where she designed and made costumes and dresses, and where she worked in clay or talked mad talk and encouraged me to do the same.

Halloween was greater than July 4th, almost greater than Christmas on our block, mainly because of Neva. She would dress me up as a witch, putting wax on my nose to make it look big and crooked, and pour candle-tallow on my fingers to turn them into witch's hands, and hide me in basements or attics to scare friends she brought in.

Every October we'd drive far out in the farm country and bring home a Tin Lizzie full of pumpkins and cornshooks from which to decorate. Neva's craziness about October infected me. A story like my "Homecoming" derives mainly from the way Neva looked at October and its ghosts and haunts.

Some Halloweens she put out all the lights in the big house and made us file in one at a time in our spook costumes, following a long ceiling-hung guideline of kite string through the rooms. The stairs going up to the attic and down to the basement were covered with partitions from the dining room table so you had to slide down these homemade chutes into darkness. Neva would vanish and reappear in various disguises during the night. There was always a beast in the basement waiting to eat you, or a monster in the attic creaking the boards, hoping for leftovers.

At around the same time I was madly in love with Aladdin and the Magic Lamp and wanted to put on a play about it. Neva cut out a paper outfit, along with a cap, and attached a pig-tail and put it on me so that I became Aladdin.

It was the Depression and we had no money. But we had books at hand. One afternoon Neva brought out a huge volume that weighed ten pounds. It was *Tales of Mystery and Imagination* by Edgar Allan Poe. I had never heard of Poe and had never seen that book. She handed it to me and said, "Young man, read this! You're going to love it. I've loved Poe all my life and now it's up to you. Lug it over to that table and open it up."

I lugged it over to the table and opened up that huge book and looked at the stories. By pure accident I turned to the page with "The Cask of Amontillado." I plunged in and got drunk immediately. I was nine years old and had never read anything like it; I fell in love completely with Edgar Allan Poe.

When I finished this story I read it again and then turned back through the book to find "The Fall of the House of Usher." The same experience happened. When Usher fell, I fell with it. I next read "The Tell-Tale Heart." For that entire day I could hardly stay away from that book. I spent eight hours reading from it and love filled my heart.

In the following weeks I read more and more Poe stories, including "The Masque of the Red Death" and "The Black Cat." All these stories influenced me, one after another, so that they filled my imagination. Later in my life, when I wrote *The Martian Chronicles*, I added the story "Usher II," because of my belief in literature. Books were being burned all over the world so I wrote "Usher II" in response and it became part of my history, leading up to my writing *Fahrenheit 451*.

Not only did Neva introduce me to Poe, but before that she introduced me to *Alice in Wonderland* and used to read the Oz books to me, which of course became a huge part of my life. When my book *The Golden Apples of the Sun* was published, I dedicated it to her, writing: "To Neva, daughter of Glinda the Good Witch."

Neva studied at the Art Institute in Chicago, and often took me there. I was amazed at everything I saw. She was the one who took me to the Chicago Century of Progress Fair in 1933. That fair made me want to grow up to be an architect. When I found out that they were going to tear down the exhibit two years later, I told Neva that I wanted to rebuild the fair. She took me home and helped me to rebuild it in the backyard. I knew that some-day I'd be an architect and build worlds of the future. (Part of this came true when I helped design the top floor of the United States Pavilion at the 1964 World's Fair in New York.)

All this because my Aunt Neva encouraged me and influenced me and loved me. She was a true artist. I can never say enough about her. I turn ninety this year. All of these memories are still strong in me. But the strongest still is my remembrance of that wonderful Poe book that she introduced me to all those years ago.

When Neva passed away a few years ago she left that book to me. I remember picking it up, lugging it over to a table, and opening it, saying, "Where are you, 'Cask of Amontillado'? Your friend is here. I want to read you."

And so I read "The Cask of Amontillado" again, for the first time in decades. In doing this I looked back and saw just how much Poe influenced me to be a writer. Because of him I wrote my first stories for *Weird Tales*. Last year, the post office came out with the Poe stamp and I ended up buying five hundred of them! I put Poe on all of my mail.

So you see how my Aunt Neva and *Tales of Mystery and Imagination* changed my life. I'm glad to preface this book to tell you how love of real books can change yours.

INTRODUCTION

Sean Manning

Look, I'm not going to say I'm not completely blown away by the cutting-edge technology of e-Readers, or that the first time I played around with the Kindle and iPad and Nook I wasn't totally geeking out. Because I am, I was. It's just that, to me, one of the best parts of reading, one of the things that hooked me— aside from Pizza Hut's "Book It!" elementary school program and my quest to help win my third-grade homeroom a pizza party—is the tactile sensation of turning a page, the sight of my bookmark inching along night after night, getting closer and closer to the finish, then finally closing the book, hearing that *whomp*, turning it over in my hands, feeling the weight of it, the sense of accomplishment that brings.

You don't get that pushing the buttons or tapping the screen of an e-Reader. You don't need a bookmark. Which, if you ask me, is one of the devices' biggest shortcomings: What are you supposed to do with your postcards and boarding passes, your concert and movie and sporting event stubs, your love notes and flower petals, funeral prayer cards and laminated obituaries?

But then that's ultimately what books themselves are—mementos, keepsakes, mile markers in one's life. Look at the titles in your e-Reader's "Library" folder. What's the most you remember about them? How long each took to download? When I glance at my shelves, I see not just multicolored rows of spines but cities where I traveled and resided, classes I took, jobs I worked, people I loved and who loved me. I see myself through the years and across the many stages of my life—my varying confidence and insecurity, ever-changing hopes and fears, all I thought I knew and still had yet to learn.

Whether it's Joyce Maynard on her father's Bible or Jonathan Miles on his mother's copy of *Ship of Fools*, Anthony Doerr on the short story anthology that kept him company while backpacking in New Zealand or Anthony Swofford on the copy of *The Stranger* he carried while soldiering in the Persian Gulf, Louis Ferrante on the edition of *Les Misérables* that helped him endure prison or Shahriar Mandanipour on the copy of *Das Kapital* that nearly landed him there (or worse), Sigrid Nunez or Rabih Alameddine on their irretrievable paperback versions of *Mythology* and *The Carpetbaggers*, Michael Ruhlman or Terrence Holt on the texts that launched their respective careers in food writing and medicine, Julia Glass on one of the first books she ever read or Jim Knipfel on the last—the authors gathered here share this appreciation for the mnemonic power of good old-fashioned books. And if you're holding this one in your hands, you likely do, too.

Now turn the page.

The Crying of Lot 49 and
In the Heart of the Heart
of the Country

JIM SHEPARD

I have this fantasy of plentitude and then of plentitude whisked away that dates from my childhood. In the summer of 1967 our family went to the World's Fair in Montreal, and back then what I may have loved more than anything else were those intricately hand-painted toy soldiers at which the Europeans excelled. I rarely saw them, because I'd never been to Europe, but I'd glimpsed them every so often on the occasional trip to one of the tonier toy stores in Manhattan. Even those stores tended to carry only a few of them. So I dreamed, when first hearing about our trip to Montreal, of stumbling across some sort of mother lode of unguessed-at riches in that regard.

My desire was fierce enough that when we first got into the city—to save money and provide ourselves with some other attractions, we were staying in one of those knotty-pine cabins on Lake Champlain, and driving the hour back and forth to the Fair—I actually maneuvered my way into a phone booth and talked my father into waiting while I checked the yellow pages for likely toy stores. I even called one or two that sounded plausible, but once they informed me that they weren't within rock-throwing distance of the street corner on which I stood, it became clear that my father wasn't going to, as he put it, drive all over the goddamned city looking for them.

In fact, he'd shied away from even driving into the city—who knew what kind of exotic street signs or miserable traffic he'd encounter?—and had parked at one of the Fair's designated outer lots, served by the city's Metro system.

So there we were, on our way home on the Metro after a long day's Fair-going, riding dully along, when suddenly at God knew what stop I looked up through the car's doors to see the dazzlingly lit and glittering toy store of my dreams. Rows upon rows of tiny, hand-painted figures, and not just the usual Napoleonic types but also Romans and Vikings and Greeks! I floated from the car in the direction of that amazing display window. I stood before it for some impossibly short amount of time. And then my father, who'd been shouting for me in an impressive panic, finally got my attention. He was in the Metro car's doorway, holding the doors open. He continued shouting until I got the idea and ducked back under his arm and into the car again.

What the Christ had I thought I was doing, he wanted to know for the next few stops. It was only then that I revived and asked frantically what stop that had been. Of course he didn't know. And then we came to our stop, and he hustled me out onto the platform.

It probably goes without saying that I never found the place again. On all my subsequent trips on the Metro, I stayed glued to my window each way and still never saw it. None of my family had seen it in the first place, as focused as they'd been on my apparent decision to get myself lost in Montreal's Underground. Were we now somehow on a different line? Had it all been a hallucination? Your guess is as good as mine. It remained in my psyche, though, as an example of how the world worked: There were amazing things out there, and every so often they appeared, in order to be all the more quickly swept away.

Two of the compensations for having accepted a tenure-track job way out in the woods of northwestern Massachusetts, I decided, were that first, and nearly instantly, I could get a dog, and second, and more gradually, I could start to collect hardcover—better—copies of those books I loved. Like most people just out of graduate school, I had a library that consisted almost entirely of paperbacks that were beat to shit, to use the technical term.

This was of course before Alibris or Amazon or any sort of Internet shopping, which meant that the only place to find a hardcover book that was not brand new was either by mail order, which seemed to me a course reserved for shut-ins, or in used book stores.

I met a new friend who was dweeby enough to have compiled a list of all the used book stores in a four- or five-hour radius, and we started hitting those places on road trips. It was a lot of fun—we'd usually end up in some ptomaine palace of a diner on the way home—but we were very quickly struck by how often we came across the same books, and how rarely we scored one of the books on our Most Wanted lists.

Every so often we'd check out such places alone, as well, and at one point it transpired that I was driving with my mother to Manhattan, and though my friend couldn't go, he had pointed out that I'd be passing right by a bookstore in Hastings-on-Hudson about which he'd heard excellent things.

It was easy to locate and looked promising at first but then nothing in particular materialized, in terms of finds. A few somewhat interesting things, but nothing I hadn't seen before. I was drifting into the nonfiction aisles in that vaguely disappointed way I would when a bookstore hadn't worked out, in the hopes that I'd still score something weird in some unexpected subcategory, when my mother, who almost never went into bookstores (I was the first in my family to go to college, and outside of work, she and my father almost never read anything other than stop signs), figured she might as well speak up for her son, since she knew her son wouldn't speak up for himself. She asked the guy behind the counter if he knew he had an author in the store.

My mother was born in southern Italy and has a voice like Anna Magnani, so even in the nonfiction section I heard her and cringed. I was cringing because I knew why she was bringing this up. Once it was established that I was an author, she was going to ask if that qualified me for some kind of discount. Everybody in the world was getting a free handout on something except her family, she believed.

"Oh really?" the guy said, polite but uninterested. "What's his name?"

My mother told him. It turned out that he was a fan, which was startling. Back then, pretty much unprecedented.

She led him to me. He shook my hand, told me how much he'd loved my third novel (which had plummeted out of print almost before my closest friends had read it), and asked if I'd sign the two books of mine that were in the store.

While I was signing them, he asked what I was looking for. I told him. He got the kind of look in his eye that Captain Nemo must have gotten when people asked him if he'd ever seen a craft that could sail underwater. "Come with me," he said.

He walked me over to a derelict-looking building across the street. He unlocked the padlock on the door, led me up the stairs and along a corridor, unlocked another padlock on some steel inner doors, and ushered me into a loft that to this day causes my breath to catch when I think back on it.

Extending in all directions were ranks of grey metal storage shelves, head-high and spanning out around me, filled with hard-cover books. Think of that famous crane shot at the end of *Raiders of the Lost Ark*, in which we realize that the crated-up Ark is now just a needle in some staggeringly large government haystack of a storage room, and you get the idea. But it got even better: Once he led me to the half of the room that held the fiction and I started heading down the rows, it was that childhood moment from Montreal all over again, only this time without the Metro's doors closing.

I not only immediately spotted pristine hardcover copies of books I'd been hunting for years—Robert Coover's *Pricksongs and Descants*, John Barth's *Lost in the Funhouse*, J. M. Coetzee's *The Life and Times of Michael K*, and Flannery O'Connor's *Collected Stories*—but also registered that there were multiple copies of each, as though the store in some gently comic way wanted to flaunt its greatness. On top of that, everything seemed priced to buy: between ten and twenty dollars. After I'd checked and double-checked those merciful numbers, I started making a pile in my arms. Very quickly I started setting my piles down in order to begin new piles. Sometimes I'd put a book back when I found two others that excited me even more. Eventually it got to the point where I thought I absolutely had to stop, even though so many more rows remained to be explored. By the half-assed running tally that I'd been keeping in my head, I figured I was now up to around five hundred dollars.

It turned out to be a little less. And in five shopping bags waiting to be toted out to the car I had thirty-eight hard-to-find and beautiful books. On what I would have previously considered a hugely successful outing to a bookstore such as this, I might have landed only one.

"I certainly hope you're going to give him a discount," my mother told the owner. He knocked off another 20 percent, making her day.

One of those shopping bags held two of the hardcovers for which I'd been searching the longest: William Gass's *In the Heart of the Heart of the Country* and Thomas Pynchon's *The Crying of Lot 49.* Gass's story collection in hardcover was compact and, in its matte-brown dust jacket with muted yellow and orange lettering, appealingly unassuming in a way that was apt and therefore aesthetically satisfying as an object. Pynchon's novel was in some ways even more unassuming in its initial aspect. Whereas the paperback had featured a Peter Max–like cartoon illustration that seemed to want to evoke from five hundred yards The Swinging Psychedelic Sixties, the hardcover offered on its dust jacket a monochromatic image of pavement, graffitied with the loop, triangle, and trapezoid that form the muted post horn of the possible secret society. Which was the more satisfying to hold in my hand? I didn't have to decide. Each had been priced as though I was the one doing the pricing.

I felt, once I'd gotten home, as if I'd rubbed the bottle and been granted thirty-eight wishes. I reread all or at least parts of each of the books, just to feel at leisure the heft of each in my hand. And of course I was very soon anxious to get back to that store. But I was heading into a brutally busy semester. I went back the first time a few months later and the store was closed, for whatever reason, and then one thing led to another and I didn't manage to return until six months or so after that.

You can see where this is going. The storefront was boarded up, the space inside empty. I asked at the local diner and was told that the owner had died and the bookstore had closed. What had happened to all of the books stored across the street? The guy at the diner hadn't known there were books stored across the street. Was there anybody I could reach to talk to about where everything went? The owner's family, the guy guessed. Did any of them live around here? Not that he knew. Did anyone know how to get in touch with them? Not that he knew.

I stood in the middle of the street, my hands on my hips. Yet for all of my disappointment, I wasn't anywhere near as bereft as

I'd been in Montreal. Not only because I'd matured—Ha!—but also because in this case I'd been allowed my time inside the charmed circle. I'd carried away all of those beautiful fictions as a result. I'd not only been allowed a glimpse at the entirety of that bounty but I'd been granted my portion, as well, if not more than my portion. That's what the physical object of a book that I love can evoke for me, and that's all anyone can ask.

Andersen's Fairy Tales

_____

FRANCINE PROSE

One winter day, three years ago, I was overcome by a sudden desire to read, or perhaps just hold in my hands, my childhood copy of *Andersen's Fairy Tales*. I knew (or thought I knew) that I still owned the book, which against all odds I had somehow managed to keep through adolescence, college, cross-country moves, the long migration from my parents' home to my own, all the usual and particular dislocations and disruptions. But I looked everywhere and couldn't find it.

Being the sort of person who, in cases like this, most often assumes the worst, I searched with rising panic and growing hopelessness, increasingly convinced that the book was gone forever. (I should explain that my library is spread out over two houses and numerous bookcases, which at that time were not arranged in any logical order. The summer before last, I finally organized some of my books according to a system that at least occasionally allows me to locate something.) Certain that the book was gone, I felt the pain one might feel when a cherished keepsake, a ring or watch, the sole remaining memento of a loved one, has, like its original owner, been lost. It hardly seemed possible that something I'd saved for fifty years could have just disappeared, but books have wills of their own. They migrate from room to room, they lend themselves to friends, they fling themselves off a shelf at us when they suspect that we need them. And if a book could vanish, *Andersen's Fairy Tales* seemed a likely candidate to have mastered that magic trick.

I missed the book *more* than a keepsake. I grieved for it as if for a person.

How beautiful the Internet is, when we turn to it, as we so often do, in our dark hours of fear and need. Within a few clicks I discovered what my childhood edition of Andersen *was*. Translated by Mrs. E. V. Lucas and Mrs. H. B. Paul, it had been published in 1945, or as the copyright page said, in MCMXLV, as part of Grosset and Dunlap's Illustrated Junior Library series, a collection of handsomely illustrated, inexpensive clothbound books for children that included *Aesop's Fables*, *A Tale of Two Cities*, *Little Women*, and *Grimm's Fairy Tales*. *Alice in Wonderland* featured the classic drawings of Tenniel, while *Robinson Crusoe*, *Swiss Family Robinson*, and *Kidnapped* were illustrated by Lynd Ward, whose picture-narrative books, like the muscular-Deco populist 1929 *God's Man*, predated the modern graphic novel by half a century.

The Andersen was illustrated by Arthur Szyk. After so many years, I remembered the images with startling clarity, and I knew that my longing for the book had as much to do with the illustrations as with Andersen's text. I wanted the Proustian moment of experiencing once again the effect that had been produced on me by the alchemical combination of the strangeness of the stories and the bright exotic pictures. I wanted to touch the object that I had so often touched as a child.

Though nothing could have consoled me for the loss of my book, it was a comfort that, with a few mouse-clicks more, I discovered that several copies were available, none of them very costly. It seemed like a bargain, a few dollars plus postage, in exchange for the restoration of a missing piece of my life.

I ordered two copies, just in case, one from each of two booksellers.

In a week or so, they arrived, encased in the padded envelopes, the bubble wrap, the unique signature of an individual's consciousness and care that is among the rewards of buying from online sellers of used books, and from eBay.

If the cover was sweetly familiar, with its wheat-colored weave stamped with green line drawings of storks and brown letter *A*'s, the endpaper was jolting, at once intimate and alienating. Seeing it was like suddenly coming upon a photo of the house in which I grew up. If so, it was a strange house, crowded and floating in space. The image has no background but a flat pale ochre behind the teeming group portrait of the principal figures with which Szyk populated Andersen's stories. On the top left is the Snow Queen, mysterious, aloof, and appropriately larger than anyone else. Beneath her is the toy ballerina, the adored love object of the Steadfast Tin Soldier, while a gremlin resembling a highly animated tree root reaches over a low wall, behind the Emperor and the Nightingale hovering like the holy spirit. On the right, past the rather attractive Ugly Duckling, sits an old man in a chair, holding a book, presumably the author, though his face more closely suggests a Polish-Jewish relative of Szyk's than the odd-looking Dane who stares at us so unhappily from photos of Hans Christian Andersen.

Szyk's images evoke medieval manuscript illumination and the miniature paintings of India and Persia. There are the same jewel-like colors, the stylized grace of the figures, the condensed fanciful narratives, the extravagant decorative patterns. In the illustration for "The Marsh King's Daughter," the part Egyptian, part Art Nouveau Princess sways her shapely arms in the huladancer tribute of an altarpiece angel; in the background are two large storks, with three more in the air, all of which could have been plucked from a row of hieroglyphics on a Pharaoh's tomb.

The East Wind from "The Garden of Paradise" is a Chinese aristocrat in silks and brocade, flying diagonally up the page and bearing on his shoulders a prince from a Netherlandish family portrait. The cowherd in "Great Claus and Little Claus" could be walking across a field in a fourteenth-century Book of Hours, while the insects and forest creatures menacing "The Girl Who Trod on a Loaf" seem like visitors from one of Bosch's nightmares. Often Szyk's birds look especially bright-eyed and crazed.

Arthur Szyk was, in his youth, a celebrated artist, honored in his native Poland, winning prizes and commissions in Morocco, France, and throughout Europe. A Jew who had fought in the Russian Army in World War I, and with the Poles against the Bolsheviks in 1921, Szyk rapidly grasped the implications of National Socialism, and anti-Nazi images and caricatures soon found their way into his work. Szyk's political stance, and the effectiveness of his cartoons, captured the attention of anti-Axis politicians and public figures, including Franklin and Eleanor Roosevelt, whose admiration was increased by a series of paintings Szyk did (in advance of Norman Rockwell's response to the same subject) illustrating "The Four Freedoms" that FDR enumerated in a State of the Union address. Though Szyk was unable to save his mother, who died in a concentration camp, he himself found refuge in the United States. He became a citizen, worked as an editorial cartoonist at the *New York Post*, and designed advertising for companies including Coca-Cola and U.S. Steel. Sadly, the wholeheartedness of Szyk's embrace by his adoptive country was short-lived. In 1949, he was investigated by the House Un-American Activities Committee. Two years later, he died of heart disease.

Of course, I didn't know any of this when I first fell under the spell of Szyk's illustrations. I would not have understood, if I had. All I knew was that, along with Andersen's stories, the pictures created a world that was brighter, roomier, full of imaginative possibility, and in every way more interesting than my own. Just as fairy tales provide a young reader with an introduction to the elements of literature—plot, characters, suspense, language, and so forth—Szyk's images offered a rudimentary lesson in art history. For a long time, I was a passionate fan of Asian miniatures and medieval manuscript illumination, and I still admire Sienese painting as much as, if not more than, any other period of art.

In a translation that even now seems crisp, eloquent, and fresh, I read and reread the stories in which Andersen kept trying so hard to shepherd his child-characters toward happy Christian futures (sun shining, birds chirping, roses blooming, children singing hymns) but kept dropping them into hells along the way (death by amputated feet; paralysis and torment by spiders, snakes, and toads; seduction and imprisonment in the Snow Queen's icy palace; abandonment on frozen city streets on New Year's Eve). Encountering Andersen's stories as an adult, I could hardly miss the dark erotic undercurrents, the terrors and anxieties, the subversive morality, the distressing frequency with which cruelty and violence are rewarded, the frustrated romantic longings stunting nearly every relationship, even those that seem unromantic. Still, each story seemed familiar, each in a different way. I remembered how partial I had been to "The Tinder Box," because I was scared of dogs, and it had pleased me to think of gigantic canines turned meek as kittens when they sat on a witch's apron. Also, because children appreciate the conceptual and rhetorical possibilities of ascending size, I had liked the idea of a dog with eyes the size of saucers, a dog with eyes the size of millstones, a dog with eyes as big as the Round Tower. How big was the Round Tower?

A few weeks after I received the substitute copies of the 1945 edition of Andersen, I found the one I thought I had lost. It was in a bookcase in the upstairs hall of my country house, not the first place I would have looked, though I was certain that I *had* looked there. Books do have wills of their own, reasons of their own, one of which would soon become clear.

The real book, as I've come to think of it, is almost impossible to distinguish from the two nearly identical impostors that had arrived in the mail. Aside from the totemic value of it having been *mine*, the only visible difference is my signature, in the upper left-hand corner of the blank page after the flyleaf, and again on the title page. My cramped practiced cursive makes me think I must have been nine or ten. Also on both pages, in the opposite corner, I've written *G-18*. I have no idea what that means, what group it signified, though (because my school had only one class per grade) it probably referred to a group in the summer day camp I attended. Does the *G* stand for girls? Most likely. Maybe I lent the book to a friend, inscribed with proof that it was mine, or contributed to a group library and wanted to ensure its return. The signature does less to connect me with the girl who belonged to G-18 than does the tale of "The Steadfast Tin Soldier" or the illustration of the full-blown roses, seated in thrones and crowned with the tiny bewigged heads of an eighteenth-century king and queen. Even so, it's *my* book, and after its first loss, I've kept it in my study, close enough for me to watch it.

The reason I can more or less precisely date the onset of my longing for the book was that it coincided with the arrival of my granddaughter into the world. The first girl in our family in a generation, she made me think back to my own childhood, a train of thought that ultimately led to *Andersen's Fairy Tales*, and to my sudden desire for the book.

In the process of trawling for copies online, I'd come across an eBay listing for a series of prints of Arthur Szyk's Andersen illustrations. I couldn't believe my good fortune, and though I should have been alerted by their extremely low price, I ordered them— only to discover that they were simply pages removed from a book much like the three copies I now owned. I decided to have six of these "prints" matted and framed, as a present for my granddaughter. It came out well. It hangs in her room. Though she is tall for a three-year-old, I still have to lift her to see the images—the Marsh King's Daughter, the king and queen of the roses, Little Tiny on a leaf. She likes the pictures. She knows them. They are part of her childhood. But it is already clear to me she will never have the same relation to the images on her wall as I had to the ones in my book.

The difference is the context in which the pictures appear, the nature of the object, a book, the way in which it is used. Seeing something from a distance and behind glass is not the same as holding it and slowly turning the pages. The way words and pictures reveal themselves as we page through a book cannot be approximated by the touch of an e-Reader button, or by gazing at them, all at once, however handsomely framed, on the wall.

That is why, in a few years, when she's a little older, I plan to give my granddaughter my copy of the 1945 Grosset and Dunlap edition of *Andersen's Fairy Tales*. And that is why it's fortunate that my own book hid from me for a while, long enough for me to have purchased, in my panic and grief, a pair of spares. Perhaps it represents the failure of a weak imagination, but I cannot quite imagine feeling the same way about passing my first e-book down to a new generation.

The Stranger

ANTHONY SWOFFORD

The Merchant of Venice, The Iliad, and *The Stranger*: a few weeks into my combat deployment to Saudi Arabia in August of 1990 my mother sent me this portable library of three. I'd requested the books in a letter home. To buy them, my mother drove from the suburbs where I grew up to downtown Sacramento. My mother is directionally challenged. She has lived in Sacramento for over thirty years. Still, to this day she will call me in New York and say, "Honey, I'm in downtown Sacramento and I'm lost. I think I'm on P Street near your old apartment. I'm looking for the co-op. Can you direct me?"

Somehow that August she found Tower Books without my assistance. I'm unsure of why I asked for *The Merchant of Venice*. *The Iliad* is pretty obvious. I wanted *The Stranger* because upon my first reading it five years before, it felt deeply subversive and countercultural, certainly counter to the culture that presently ruled every moment of my day, every cell of my body: the U.S. military assembled in the Persian Gulf, the most wicked and powerful military yet assembled for warfare. I was a minor player in this maximal theater of war.

The cover of the paperback featured trippy and mysterious blue and black imagery reminiscent of the opening credits of a James Bond film. There was the postage stamp–size image of a man on a sizzling beach and the Vintage International moniker that signified the book meant something, that it had done tours through the academy, that the writer had made a difference, made a mark on the world. Though it rarely rained in the desert, I carried it and the other two books in Ziploc bags. This didn't keep sand from invading their spines and pages.

Meursault—"Monsieur Antichrist," as his judge would later dub him—whipped up my anti-religion fervor and further encouraged my effort to be listed as "No Religion" on my dog tags, thus far an administrative dead-end. It was as if the Pope himself was against me on this one. But I had Albert Camus on my side. He would be with me in my fighting hole, not a Roman Catholic God.

And because Meursault on one afternoon had floated with his beautiful Marie in the hot seawater, and had fondled her breasts and then made love to her (within two pages!), and because later he'd killed a man on the beach, an Arab man, for apparently no reason, and had gone to his death with no regrets, I admired him. I esteemed his stoicism in the face of calamity. At twenty I looked around the desert, at the machinery of war, at the very real possibility that I'd be required to kill men and then have to walk away from the deed and try to reenter society. Religion held no answers. Camusian absurdism did.

Just as chance had put Meursault on that beach, with a pistol in his hand, chance had put me in the Arabian Desert, with a rifle in mine. I could have ended up on a submarine base pulling guard duty. I could have ended up as a typist at the Marine Corps administrative headquarters in Kansas City. It was not a question of right or wrong, of good or bad, but rather of being. As Meursault might say, there was no use in thinking about it—it simply was.

So the desert became my home, and my rucksack became my library, and I carried Albert Camus with me, the way others carried their Bibles and their Clancy. When camouflage Bibles were handed out and I left mine behind at a rear-area barracks, I got strange looks from my comrades. Granted, the Bibles were thicker than *The Stranger*, they'd be more likely to stop that one in a million bullet every God-loving soldier hopes to be saved from with scriptural ink, but I had more faith in a dead French writer from forty years prior than in a dead miracle worker from twenty centuries ago. And in all of the reading I'd done in the Bible, and all of the scripture I'd heard over the years sitting through Mass, I never came across any discussion of Jesus swimming with a beautiful girl in the ocean and getting her into bed in two pages. When you're twenty, sex always beats salvation, by a landslide.

So *The Stranger* became my pornography there in the desert. Meursault and Marie are in a movie theater after their encounter on the beach:

> She had her leg pressed against mine. I was fondling her breasts. Towards the end of the show, I gave her a kiss, but not a good one. She came back to my place.
> When I woke up Marie had gone.

There was more sensuality and dread and sex and release in those five sentences, in that paragraph break alone, than I could have gathered from every hidden pornography stash in the entire desert. Legs. Breasts. A kiss, but not a good one—the great fear of every inexperienced lover—I have failed early and now I will lose the long game, she knows I can't kiss, she knows I will be horrible in bed. But no! The desired woman does come home with the hapless man. In the morning only the memory of her remains, in the bed, in the sheets, between the lines. And the pursuer will shortly become the pursued.

This might not be a very sophisticated reading of one of the most important philosophical novels of the twentieth century. But it is one way into the novel, and one way into all of literature:

an on-the-ground, in-your-face physicality that the best books possess. Gravitas and pathos and thanatos and eros crammed into small, black marks on thin, flimsy pieces of paper.

Books. Lives.

That paperback copy of *The Stranger* my mother mailed to me in the desert cost her $5.95. It was the first Vintage International Edition, from March of 1989. I graduated from Marine Corps boot camp in March of 1989. This is a coincidence, certainly, but one that thrills. During the winter of '88–'89, while I marched around the parade ground and rifle range and sand pits where drill instructors sculpted sloppy and undisciplined boys into full-fledged killers of men, a group of kindly publishing people in New York City spent their days moving Matthew Ward's masterful new translation from hardcover into paperback, readying it for spring publication.

Another coincidence: While working on this essay, I found a thirteenth printing of *The Stranger* in my girlfriend's parents' bookshelves at their house in Connecticut. It cost $15.95, but that was the only discrepancy. The cover and fine translation were the same. At Sarah's parents' kitchen table I set down my sand- and war-battered copy next to this newer volume and checked the pagination of the sexy paragraph break above. In both versions it appeared on pages 20 and 21.

Yet the two books could not be more different. The spine of my copy is mightily worn; there are a few places where the wear and tear runs into the letters in the title—the *E* in *THE* is scratched a bit, there is a fissure between the two title words, the *C* in *CAMUS* is underlined with a faint scratch. Throughout the pages are my marginalia and stains and history.

For me, forever, this beaten-up copy I dragged around in my rucksack for nine months will always be a badge of my awakening as a writer. I'd wanted to be a writer since my teens, since discovering Camus and Hemingway and Steinbeck, all of the male writers who make hot-blooded American boys want to become writers. But I'd never been tested, intellectually or physically or morally. At war I was tested every day. I walked away from war wanting only to forget it. But like the glint of Meursault's pistol on that burning beach, the glint of the pistol that blinded him before he fired his shots into the Arab, my experience in that burning desert altered me, changed me as a writer and a man. Perhaps it even made me a writer; it certainly made me a different writer from the one I'd have become if I'd gone to university at eighteen or become a carpenter, another option at the time. That battered copy of *The Stranger* that I carried around the desert was an integral part of my writer's education.

Books mean different things each time we read them. I go back to *The Stranger* every year or so, sometimes twice a year if I need a quick fix, a reminder of a youthful angst and hatred that are fashionable when young but that wear out as one ages. That weekend up at Sarah's parents' house, I read my copy late at night while she was asleep next to me in bed. We'd just had a wonderful week in our nascent relationship. She'd been in Paris for the ten days prior, and when she returned our feelings blossomed, grew in ways that neither of us had expected. On the verge of falling into a big romantic love, a new life, the old tattered book seemed to belong to my long ago past—to the machismo and fright of my twenties, not to a steady and loving forties and beyond.

In the morning I woke up and she was still there.

Speak, Memory

DANIELLE TRUSSONI

I don't know where I bought *Speak, Memory*, or even if I bought it at all. It came into my life during my sophomore year in college, when I was working at a bookstore in Madison, Wisconsin. Often I would discover books at work, buy them at a discount, and bring them home. Perhaps this is how *Speak, Memory* came into my possession. But I suspect it was instead a gift from a man I was dating, someone who had crates of poetry books in the back of his beat-up Ford and a tendency to write his thoughts in ink on the pages of these books, inscribing them around each straggling line of free verse, inking over the words of his favorite poets with a ballpoint pen. Or perhaps the book wasn't a gift at all. Perhaps I knew the relationship with this particular boyfriend would never go beyond poetry and late-night drives and—in a moment of spite—I stole the book from him. I imagine myself taking the book from one of the boxes in the backseat of the car, noticing that it wasn't a book of poems but a memoir by the man who had written *Lolita* and, after tucking it into my bag, deciding that I would never speak to the boy again. At nineteen, I still held onto the illusion that stealing a man's book was the next best thing to stealing his heart. I know now, of course, that it's much, much better.

Looking over my copy I can see that there is nothing special in the book's appearance. It is here on my desk as I write, its cover bent and ragged. My favorite book isn't a first edition, or even a hardbound copy with a dust jacket. It is a much-abused Vintage paperback with a photograph of Nabokov in the hollow of a rowboat, oars crossing his body, sunlight falling upon the leaves of what looks like an oak tree, although the quality of the photograph makes it a bit difficult to identify. The spine is broken, the pages dog-eared and water-stained. Simply picking it up and turning it in my hands allows me to remember the years I have spent with it.

The water stains came about from my habit of reading *Speak, Memory* in the bath. I would fill the tub to the very top with scalding water, ease in, and prop up the book on the cold porcelain edge. At moments of intense concentration or enjoyment, I would allow the book to slip down under the steamy liquid surface. The thirsty paper absorbed the water, soaking it up until the book became slightly heavier in my hand, alerting me to my lapse. I did this many times, as I love to read in the bathtub and I reread *Speak, Memory* each year. Over time, the paper has become brittle, and it is not beyond the realm of imagination that, one of these days, I will turn the pages and they will deteriorate in my fingers, the paper crumbling to a dust as fine as the coating of a moth's wing. Sometimes it seems that the objects one loves can be more fragile, more prone to disintegration, than memory itself.

Losing my copy of *Speak, Memory* would be particularly difficult. I love the physicality of the book, and all the markings I've made upon it. There are passages written over with pencil, pagecorners I've turned, a folded grocery list used as a bookmark. I open to the photographs of Nabokov's relatives before they were exiled from Russia. They are a grand bourgeois family, everyone impeccably dressed. There is another photo of Nabokov's wife, Vera, and their son, Dmitri, standing outside an apartment building. And yet another of Nabokov's cramped writing desk, his pens and papers spread before him. It is always something of a shock to see these images of the "real" Nabokov, as they crowd into the imaginary ones I've created over the years.

On the back cover of the book, there is a note that says "Photography: Courtesy of the Estate of Vladimir Nabokov," and this leaves me to imagine not some legal entity doling out permissions to reprint photographs but a vast stone and marble mansion that holds all of the images and keepsakes of my favorite writer. There would be a great hallway filled with portraits in oil; a drawing room holding the objects he took with him when he left Russia at age nineteen; a cigar room with a glass case containing the butterflies he collected in Switzerland during the last decade of his life; a desk holding a few papers he graded as an instructor at Cornell; a long wooden trestle table in a dim-lit library displaying the many thousands of note cards he used to forge first drafts. The photograph on the cover of my abused paperback—the magical picture of Nabokov rowing a wooden boat under the canopy of an oak tree—would be hung in Vera's dressing room, where she could gaze at her husband at the height of his youth and beauty, his eye meeting the camera with interest, something bordering upon suspicion, as if he wished to capture the camera as much as it wished to capture him.

My adventures have always included *Speak, Memory*. It has come with me to many places in the United States, but also to Japan and to England and to Bulgaria and to France, each time being packed, unpacked, shelved, and read. I have read *Speak, Memory* in a tiny o-furo-style bathtub in Yoshii, Japan; on a park bench in Iowa City, USA; on a great white couch in my apartment in Sofia, Bulgaria; and on the beaches near Montpellier, France. It is the book that I have always brought with me, the one that I did not donate to a library or sell to a used book store or give to a friend, the one that I reread once I'd unpacked my things and settled in. Perhaps it has become an object of good luck, or one that signals that I've made a new home. It was the book that made me feel less foreign in the foreign places I chose to live. How strange, I think as I look at it, that this object has become a kind of bridge between my past and future.

I sometimes wonder if I have carried *Speak, Memory* with me on my travels because I identified with Nabokov's itinerant life—he left Russia in 1919 and never lived there again. He moved to Berlin, Paris, New York, and, finally, Lausanne, Switzerland, writing and publishing books in each new country, changing languages as he went. It is more likely, however, that I brought *Speak, Memory* with me on my own peregrinations simply because I loved the familiar cadences of Nabokov's words, the way his sentences played in my mind when I read them. Nabokov, it is often said, is a writer's writer. And although I felt the compulsion to write from a very early age—indeed, it was a maddening feeling akin to the temptation to scratch the subtle sting of a mosquito—I only really fell in love with the possibilities of language after I discovered Nabokov's novels.

Of course *Speak, Memory* isn't a novel, although it isn't exactly an autobiography of the usual kind, either. Nabokov wasn't interested in outlining a timeline of events or even in recording the facts of his existence for his readers. Rather, he writes that he is devoted to the thematic structures of his life, to those events that have the marvelous aspect of the timeless, whether it be finding a butterfly in Switzerland identical to one he found in Russia fifty years before or reveling in the seeping, sensual presence of the synesthesia he shared with his mother. Taking the single memory from the stream of experiences, polishing it and placing it under a spotlight, rescuing it from the eddies of everyday happenings, and proclaiming that this is what matters in a life is a project I find beautiful and reassuring. In the end, it is the singular moment that triumphs. In the end, we can save our memories from the destructive wash of time.

Surely there will be no saving my copy of *Speak, Memory*. I have recently moved to France and, in the process of setting up an office in my new house, unpacked my books and set them on my writing desk. There are dictionaries and nineteenth-century novels and a few books of poetry, all in varying states of disrepair. Many of my books are well worn, but *Speak, Memory* is falling apart. The spine is shedding pages and the front cover is ready to fall away. I take it and place it next to the pristine notebooks I have stacked up, notebooks in which I hope to outline a novel, and I wonder if I should replace the paperback with a newer copy, perhaps try to find a first edition or at least a hardbound copy that might withstand the hardships I impose upon it. But a clean copy of *Speak, Memory* wouldn't be at all the same. It would be too free of my presence, too clear of the traces I have left upon each page. It would be as if the years of carrying *Speak, Memory* with me had not occurred at all.

The Shadow of the Sun

NICK FLYNN

1

Hubert Sauper gave it to me, in Paris. *The Shadow of the Sun*. It was on his shelf. He pulled it down and handed it to me, said I should have it, said it was mine. Hubert is like that.

2

It is entirely possible that he didn't give it to me, but that I bought it on his recommendation.

3

Hubert was surprised I hadn't read Kapuscinski. Or maybe I had. Something. Years ago. I might have even said, when asked if I knew him, *Kapuscinski? I know* of *him.*

4

I wince, years later, hearing Bart Simpson, when asked if he knows his multiplication tables: *The multiplication tables? I know* of *them.*

5

It must have been on one of the planning trips I took to Paris before going to Tanzania. Hubert was in the early stages of making a documentary film, the working title of which was *Darwin's*

Nightmare. The plan was to meet up in Mwanza, on the south coast (shore?) of Lake Victoria.

6

Lake Victoria, a guidebook told me, was (is) the second-largest freshwater lake in the world, the size of Israel. Or Ireland. The kind of detail that has somehow stayed with me.

7

Darwin's Nightmare was to be about guns and fish and globalization. Hubert spoke of it with a certain fervor, and his excitement was contagious. Many had said they wanted to join him, to be a part of it, but only two or three of us actually made it, over the years it took him to shoot the film.

8

Years later he told me that he never really thought I'd come.

9

The plan was I would fly to Dar es Salaam, meet my friend Deborah, who is based there, working as an international public health doctor (*daktari*). I would spend a few weeks with her, during which time Hubert would firm up his plans and let me know when he'd land in Mwanza.

10

What I didn't know was that our meeting up was based on Hubert being able to raise the money to continue with the filming.

11

To get from Dar to Mwanza, Hubert insisted I take a train. *It should be amazing*, he said, though he'd never done it. The train from Dar to Mwanza ran only twice a week, and the trip took three days.

12

I took a ferry to Zanzibar a few days after landing in Dar, to study Swahili for ten days, which isn't really enough time to learn a language, but it did allow me to stumble along.

13

I could say, a few weeks later, in perfect Swahili, after a territorial rat attempted to leap on my face, deflected only by my hand: *The only good rat is a dead rat.*

14

In a Zanzibar bazaar, surrounded by ten Muslims, less than a year after 9/11, as I looked at an Osama Bin Laden scarf, I was asked whether I liked Osama. It was tense for a moment, before I answered, *No, I don't like Osama, but I don't like Bush either*, and everyone laughed. I bought the scarf.

15

I can remember reading *The Shadow of the Sun* in a guesthouse in Zanzibar, so I must have been given it (or bought it) before I flew to Dar. Unless I found it somehow in Dar.

16

I remember a whole chapter about Zanzibar, in the early 1960s, just as the pan-African movement for independence was being argued and ironed out. I drank tea on the same hotel terrace in Dar where all the players—Nyerere, Karume, Okello, Nkrumah— imagined the postcolonial future of Africa.

17

I realized that I'd read an excerpt of it in the *New Yorker* a couple years earlier, which had also stayed with me, vividly—much more vividly, apparently, than the details of how the book came to be mine. It concerned Kapuscinski's time spent in Lagos (I think it was Lagos), choosing to live in that sprawling city among the local people for months on end. He did this partly out of necessity, as he didn't have much money to rent where the other Westerners did.

18

A story I remember is that of the alleyway outside his apartment in Lagos, where each of his neighbors owned only one thing, and he or she had to make that one thing their work. The man who owned a shirt could become a guard at the bank, the woman who owned a kettle could make tea, the man who owned a pot could cook rice to sell. One day the man who owned the pot awoke to find it gone, and he went mad, wailing his loss, knowing that the one thing that kept him alive with dignity, that kept him from simply begging, had been stolen.

19

When I'm traveling I read books written by those who are from or have lived in the country I am visiting (Homer in Greece, Joyce in Ireland, Duras in Paris, Catullus in Egypt), or by those who have spent more time there than I ever will.

20

Kapuscinski spent his whole life traveling, much of it in Africa.

21

It isn't the kind of book that names what one expects when one goes to Africa. There is very little naming of large animals, which is the question I was most asked if I told a stranger I'd been to Tanzania: *Which big animals did you see? Elephants? Wildebeests?* The biggest was that rat, which leapt for my face one night while I was under my mosquito net, trying to sleep.

22
One elephant does appear in the book, wandering through a camp, knocking over tents, if I am remembering it right.

23
I also remember a story about a pothole outside of Onitsha that was so big that trucks trying to get into the city would have to drive to the bottom of it, as there was no other way to pass. An entire network of businesses had grown up around this enormous hole: the men with the rope to haul the truck out; the women selling soda to the drivers; the police who sat on a box watching the whole event unfold, and then unfold again, and again. It went on for years. It seems purely apocryphal, until you are in Africa, and then it seems entirely plausible.

24
The world will go on there long after the Western world has come to a standstill, the day the last drop of oil is burned.

25
It was the kind of place where a book had value. When you were sitting in a café, say, waiting for the camera batteries to charge, because the next morning you'd be shooting at dawn. So your entire job is to sit and drink Coca-Cola all day. And read.

26
I had been on Chole, an island about two hundred miles south of Zanzibar, for three weeks, working with Deborah on an anemia

eradication project. Chole has no phones, electricity, cars, water, or roads. When we got back to Dar, I was expecting an e-mail from Hubert telling me where to meet him in Mwanza, but there was no e-mail. It was the date we had agreed upon, and the train was leaving the next morning, the next one not for several days. I was in the train station, in line to buy my ticket, when I felt how tired I was, how it was time to go home. I went to the airline office and changed my flight so I could leave the next day. By the time I landed in Paris the train I was to be on had crashed, killing two hundred people, injuring eight hundred more. I called Hubert from the airport, and he was home, shaken. I'd heard about it before I got on the plane; it was big news. Hubert had heard about it as well, and for a few hours, as long as it took me to fly home, he believed I was on it.

27

A few months later I made it to Mwanza. By then Hubert had the money to finish his film, which would go on to be nominated for an Academy Award for Best Documentary Feature.

28

A mango tree in a village outside of Mwanza. Someone had begun to chop it down, for firewood more than likely. It was a magnificent tree. Its shade would cool all who sat beneath it, and its fruit could feed the whole village. But one also needs a fire to cook rice, to boil water for tea.

29

A modest proposal: Certain books should exist only as e-books. These are the books that are not objects, but merely information. The books whose writers forget that language is a plastic material, that the book is sculptural. Most poetry books understand this. A John Grisham–type book doesn't. A John Grisham–type book will work just fine as an e-book—we really don't need to kill any more trees for John Grisham. Or for the biography of a former president. This says nothing about the worth of either of these types of books. It's just that they tend to end up unopened, or as landfill, after a year or two anyway. A book of poetry—a *good* book of poetry—is something you return to. If it's worthwhile, poetry uses language in a way that pulses on the page, that is alive. It is harder to bury a living thing.

The Bible

JOYCE MAYNARD

I am attached to many possessions: a pair of cowboy boots I've owned for close to thirty years and resoled more times than I can remember, stones from places I have traveled, my collection of state plates assembled from years of haunting New Hampshire yard sales and currently lacking only North Dakota and Delaware. I hold on to certain vinyl record albums from my teens (including—until one of my sons raided my collection—the original banned version of the Beatles' *Yesterday and Today*). But books, not so much. And this is odd, no doubt, given my line of work.

Maybe because I'm a person for whom the words themselves—not the pages on which they're printed or the covers that bind them—are what hold value, I am mostly unsentimental about possessing a particular copy of a book I love. When one edition of *Pride and Prejudice* gets worn out, I just pick up another in some used book store, same as I did when I misplaced my original *Will You Please Be Quiet, Please?* (though it was a first edition) and (in a different mood) *Blueberries for Sal.*

In all my lifetime of reading, there may be only one book I have ever hungered to possess as a physical object. I don't own this book, and I haven't laid eyes on it for thirty years. Still I doubt it would be an exaggeration to say that at least once a week, the wish that I could hold this book in my hands and turn its pages comes over me. And when it does, I'm struck by a sharp wave of sadness and regret. The book is my father's Bible.

I can think of no way of conveying what this book means to me without first offering a few words concerning the Bible's original owner. Twenty-eight years after my father's death—having now lived longer without him than I did with him—I find the images that remain of him have burned down to a small but powerful few. Laid out together, they form a portrait of the man as I knew him.

I see him standing on the edge of our town pool—the only father (the only person in our whole town most likely) to wear a suit of the old-fashioned style, a relic from his British youth, with a top covering his chest—instructing me in how to swim the crawl. In his fifties when I was born, my father remained a beautiful swimmer.

I see him on those Saturday mornings we went sketching together—walking side by side through the New Hampshire countryside, each of us brandishing a walking stick. His, he would raise to the sky now and then, a signal to freeze and cease all conversation as he commanded me to study the particular way the light hit a patch of grass, or a cloud formation, or a certain stand of trees.

"Listen, Chum," he whispered, in a manner that commanded reverence. He had detected the song of a warbler. Or a thrush. Possibly (though this was rare) a lark. He knew all their voices, and whistled back to them.

I see him in his attic studio, palette knife in hand, surveying a piece of masonite on which he would be painting—large, bold, beautiful but not remotely representational landscapes, inspired by the places we went on our walks and sketching trips. Making art was not how my father made his living—he worked as a teacher—but the urgency for doing so burned at the center of his life every day. And every night.

I see him in our living room, listening to a recording of Mozart's horn concertos, scratched from much playing. He is conducting the music from the chair with wild, passionate gestures. His eyes are damp; Mozart has this effect on him, particularly when combined with vodka.

I have no image of my father drinking, but many of him drunk. Lurching from one half-finished painting to another, moving pieces of construction paper on the board—should it go here, or here, what did I think? He was a man in love with color, with paint on canvas, lines on paper, forms, and the spaces between forms. His paintings consumed him, but hardly anybody in our town or anyplace else ever saw them besides my mother, my sister, and me. Mostly these viewings took place during late nights in our attic. Mostly, under the influence of alcohol.

There was a question he would ask of people who came to our house, possibly an old friend but equally likely a random acquaintance—or, most horrifyingly, my sixteen-year-old boyfriend, come to pick me up for a night at the movies. My date was not yet through the threshold of our door before I heard my father speak the familiar words.

"Tell me, my good man," he said to the boy I hoped would be my boyfriend, in a voice whose timbre and inflection could have served him well on the stage, "What is the definition of Beauty?"

Silence.

And then there is this one other image I hold of my father, all these long years since the last time I heard his voice. So many years later, in fact, that I am now myself close to the age he must have been when I first registered this picture of him.

It's early morning, possibly not even six o'clock, but he is up and dressed—a heartbreakingly handsome man, who managed to look dapper even though his clothes tended to be a little shabby. He rises before the sun, and because I am his daughter, and I adore him, and I know he believes that when the sun gets up so should I, I am coming down the stairs to start my day with him. He is sitting at our dining room table, eating his poached egg and toast. There is a book on either side of his plate. One is a heavy, oversized volume called *The Loom of Art*, filled with reproductions of paintings from the Louvre—from before the Italian Renaissance up through the Impressionists. Mornings like these, my father may study a single image for whole minutes. Possibly the entire meal. He is always checking art books out of the library, but this one we own, and because we don't own many, he knows every image as well as he knows my face.

The other book I see before him on the table contains no illustrations. The print on the pages is impossibly small, even for my young eyes, and surely must strain his, except he is so familiar with the words that he barely needs to read them. This book is the Bible—King James version, Old Testament and New. And though it has been decades since my father worshipped at a church, and longer since he would have spoken of himself as a believer—though he is married (problematically) to a Jewish woman—it is this book he values more than any other in our household. More than Milton, Elliot, Spenser, Yeats, or even the poetry of William Blake, though in his deep, melodious voice he recites to me "Little Lamb, who made thee?" every night when he puts me to bed. If—in our household filled with books—a fire were to threaten us, and there was only time to retrieve a single volume, it would be his Bible my father would reach for.

Yet it is also the book that represents everything my father tried to leave behind him long ago when he left home—and never could. As much as my father loved the Bible, he despaired of its hold on him. And because I grew up the daughter of a man who was powerfully conflicted in his relationship to that book, I carried my own brand of ambivalence about it.

"You know, Chum," he says to me often on these mornings. "You really need to read the Bible."

"Mmm," I might say before turning back to my Nancy Drew.

My father was the son of British missionaries, born in India, in a little outpost somewhere in the south of that country, where his minister father and fellow Salvation Army follower mother had come, from England, to spread the word of the Lord. His parents had eventually left the Salvation Army because its practices and creed had come to seem too liberal, and joined instead a sect known as the Plymouth Brethren who believed that a person needed one book and one book only to get through this lifetime on earth.

My father was a naturally curious person, hungry for the world and eager to experience what he called "the life of the senses" that his own stern parents disdained and prohibited. Even as a child, he sought out music and literature and most of all art, and was punished severely when he went against his father's bidding and secretly purchased—with his life savings—a paintbox.

I cannot begin to fathom how it could be that the images an eight-year-old boy made in his sketchbook with a dime-store box of paints could be viewed as the devil's work. But I suppose in the world of the Plymouth Brethren any endeavor that took a person away from studying the Bible was an endeavor to avoid. The paints were confiscated.

That story, more than any other of his childhood, captured my imagination during my own growing-up years. No fairy tales for my father, or Greek mythology, or Norse fables. But he knew the Bible inside out, and could recite the Psalms and long passages from the Old Testament. He never lost his love of it, though he left the church young—abandoned the teachings of his family and the tight constraints religion had placed on him to become a modern artist. It was a book he studied all his life.

My father didn't simply read his Bible. He remained engaged in a sixty-some year conversation with its authors. And so his copy—the one he took out every morning at breakfast—was not simply well worn but heavily annotated. I doubt there was a page in that book on which he had not written some comment or observation. Generally many.

Along with that question—"What is Beauty?"—there was a line he delivered to me at least a hundred times over the years of my growing up—two lines, actually. He told me regularly that I needed to develop a good crawl stroke. He told me with even greater frequency that I needed to read the Bible.

I had better things to do, of course. To a ten-, or twelve-, or fourteen-year-old girl—or a twenty-one-year-old, or a twenty-five-year-old—studying the Bible was as undesirable an activity as learning to play bridge, or embarking on a course in embalming. Like most young people of my day, I sought out what was entertaining and diverting and popular. There was no place in my life for boils and pestilence, women cast out by their husbands for the failure to conceive offspring, and the sacrificing of goats. I had rock and roll to occupy me. Clothes. Movies. Getting into college and figuring out who I was in the world. I wanted to explore the stuff of real life—not some dusty out-of-date story from long ago.

The year after I left home, my parents' marriage had ended, and my father—now an advanced alcoholic, but still painting daily, and still a man in possession of devastating charm and a kind of wild and raging brilliance—took up with a student of his, forty-five years younger than he. They moved to a house in the country and she became his sketching companion. They moved to England, but things did not go well. They moved back to New Hampshire and they parted, violently.

His life spun more and more out of control after that—with middle-of-the-night phone calls to me when things with her got impossible, when he was desperate. The girlfriend was going crazy. There was no money. His health was failing. The world was a mess. Where, where, where in all of this lay Beauty?

Married now, with children of my own to raise, I saw him only a few times a year after that. He was thinner than me now, with every bone in his skull visible, though he still sported those jaunty ascots of his and took walks with his sketching pad and stick, quoting poetry and noting the songs of birds along the way. And he still painted.

At the age of seventy-three, he moved out to the west coast of Canada and was recognized at last as an artist in a small but significant way by first one gallery there and then others. He was celebrated with a one-man show. He joined AA, where his testimony was, I'm told, an unfailing inspiration to all who struggled for sobriety.

When I was twenty-seven, my father came down with pneumonia. He had been sober for a while but had a relapse, went on a bender, and it did him in. He died a few months shy of his eightieth birthday, leaving stacks of sketchbooks and several hundred beautiful paintings, a few art books, a dozen natty ascots and fedoras, and drawers full of art supplies.

From three thousand miles away I came for the funeral, and to assist in what is known as putting the affairs in order—though how is a person to put in order a life that never was?

The paintings—after my sister and I made our personal selections—were consigned to a gallery. The clothing was given away. My father had been living those last years in a single room at an old persons' residence hotel. He owned almost nothing.

It took no more than a few hours to clean out his room. There was a twelve-steps manual and an unfamiliar-looking Bible. When I asked about his old one—the one I grew up with, in which he'd written all his life—nobody could find it.

"I think he gave it to Susan years ago," one of my father's friends told me. Meaning the girlfriend.

I registered the news with more shock than I would have ever guessed, and more than that, a terrible and crushing sense of loss. All my life my father had urged me to read the Bible. Knowing I had never done this, he had quoted from it as liberally as a lawyer might invoke the constitution. But in the end, it was not I, his well-loved younger daughter, but this strange interloper who had taken off with his most precious book. Maybe he'd given up on my ever opening it. Maybe he'd given up on the possibility that I'd ever know real wisdom or enlightenment, or even seek it out. Maybe he'd lost all hope somewhere along the line.

I could have purchased my own Bible, of course. It is never difficult to find a copy of the King James edition. There's been one in nearly every hotel room I've ever spent a night. But it wasn't simply the Bible I wanted. It was my father's voice, speaking to me, his only Chum, from those oft-thumbed pages, and offering up his vision of what mattered in this life—as he had all those years when I'd taken his voice so for granted, and, too often, registered only impatience and annoyance with what he said.

And here I am. Close to three decades have passed since my father died, but he remains a daily presence, and only in part because the walls of the house I live in are covered with the art he made. In my fifties now, I wonder: Which were the Psalms he loved best? Which of the disciples? What were the stories he underlined, and the comments he would have written beside them in the margins in his fine, elegant artist's hand? What pages did he turn to in those most brutal times, for solace and comfort? Where are the words that might offer me guidance now?

It would please my father to know I've developed a reasonable crawl stroke. Not as strong or rhythmic as the stroke he executed, cutting cleanly across the water of our town pool, half a century ago, when I was little, back when he taught me how to swim. Still, if there is a place of worship for me, it is probably the pool where I go, early mornings before the sun comes up, to swim my laps and meditate.

As for my father's other wish for me: I have yet to read the Bible, and though it's a poor excuse to say this is because I do not own the copy that I wish I did, it's the excuse I give, because only by reading his copy would I hear his voice speaking to me.

And then there is that question, the one that seeks to define beauty. Drunk or sober, my father asked it all his life. It has only recently occurred to me that I never asked him what he believed the answer to be. Had I asked, I think his response would have probably contained the word God.

Les Misérables

LOUIS FERRANTE

In the early '90s, I was indicted by the FBI, Secret Service, and Nassau County Prosecutor's Office, charged with heading my own crew in the Gambino Crime Family. After several years of court proceedings, I pled guilty. I'd serve my federal sentence first, followed by my state sentence.

At the beginning of my sentence my mind was mobbed up. I lived and breathed mafia life, the only life I knew. But something mysterious happened to me while serving my time. During a trip through solitary confinement, I began to think, and suddenly had regrets about the life I'd lived. With plenty of questions about the purpose of life and no one around to answer them, I turned to books. For me, it was a monumental discovery, opening up a new world to me. I'd finally found an escape from the hell of prison. I fell in love with reading, began to see things differently, and left the mob.

I was locked away with my books for over six years when at last the Federal Bureau of Prisons handed me over to the New York State penal system where I was to serve another two years. Before being sent to an upstate prison, I was locked up for several months in Long Island's Nassau County Jail. The joint was a real shit hole. Dark, dirty, and damp. Mice and cockroaches. Rapists and molesters everywhere—creeps I didn't see much of in the feds.

Upon arrival, I was put in 72-hour lockdown, an isolation cell where every con is monitored to make sure he doesn't have any diseases that can spread around the prison. For a drug addict, it's a place to kick his habit, three days to clean the dope out of his system so he can function like the rest of us normal lunatics.

I was bored and depressed. I needed a book to lift me out of the gloom, but my books had been taken from me along with my few other belongings during the prison transfer. Time drags in jail; without something to read, every day feels like a week.

I was boxed up next to a young junkie who was kicking. He screamed and cried all night long. In the morning, he moaned that he was freezing. From where I lay in my cell, I could see his bare feet shivering. His legs were too long for his bunk; his feet hung off the edge, through the bars.

I asked him if he wanted my socks. He did, and I gave them to him. I've never forgotten how polite he was, his voice stuttering through chattering teeth as he thanked me repeatedly.

By the end of the second day, he had kicked the dope, and we were both released after the third day. Another lost soul I'd never see again. Much more than the violence, loneliness, and isolation, the countless lost souls you encounter is what truly establishes prison as a hell on earth. I often wonder how many of the lives I ran across have ended in tragedy.

After 72-hour lockdown, guards designate you to a tier block where you live among the general population. I anticipated the typical tier block bullshit. Every prison is filled with predators, cons looking to strong-arm some newjack who's visibly afraid and doesn't know the ropes. To overcome them, you have to prove yourself.

Sometimes, I had to prove myself in federal prison, but not usually. Most mobsters serve time in the feds. The mafia is a close-knit society, so I was well known in most fed joints. A mafia welcoming committee generally awaited me wherever I was sent. But there aren't many mobsters in county jails, so no one knew me. Here, I was like anyone else.

It was early evening, shortly before lock-in, when I was released onto my tier block. A few gangbangers, probably Crips or Bloods, were playing cards. The chief Big Mouth said, "Yo, little man, come over here, I wanna ask you somethin.'"

I clenched my fists. "Who the fuck you callin' little man?"

Not the response Big Mouth had expected.

"Shit," he said, shaking his head, "thought you was a newjack."

"I'm down six years, motherfucker!" I jabbed a thumb into my chest. "You're new to me."

I hated talking this way but knew when to turn it on. These punks were probably serving a county bullet, a ten-month sentence. To them, six years is an eternity; I had instant respect.

A short time later, I was locked in for the night. I tossed and turned, couldn't fall asleep. I was so lost without a book, my trusted means of escape. I wanted to read so desperately that I used the dim light shining in from the corridor to read the graffiti on the cinder blocks. It seemed every con who passed through my cell had scrawled an angry or bitter remark across the walls. I waited the entire night for the bars to open so I could visit the prison library in the morning.

Shortly after chow, the hack on duty gave me a library permit. I walked in, looked around, and was pleasantly surprised. Most prison libraries keep a stock of worn, musty, out-of-print books, usually the discarded leftovers from public libraries or someone's attic. This library had a whole section of classic literature in fair condition. Most of the titles I had already read, but just seeing them on the shelves gave me the same warm feeling as walking into a room and spotting a group of old friends. Dickens, Defoe, and the Brontë sisters. Stendhal, Dumas, and Cervantes. I felt at home, even in this hell.

The first classic I noticed that I hadn't yet read was *Les Misérables*. I knew what to expect from the author, Victor Hugo, since I'd read his *Notre-Dame de Paris*. I slid the paperback from the shelf—thick like a solid brick, an unabridged edition, nearly fifteen hundred pages. I liked the cover art, and the spine was wide enough for a small sketch of a street urchin holding a broom. I signed the book out and rushed back to my cell.

When I first discovered books, I was a slow reader and had to keep a dictionary close at hand. By now, I was able to devour a three-hundred-page book in one day, seldom breaking to look up a word. *Les Mis* should've taken me about five days to finish.

Once I started, though, I began to slow my pace. I read pages and paragraphs over, sometimes chapters; Hugo's brilliance was something to be absorbed deliberately. I'd read plenty of histories about Napoleonic times, yet Hugo's ability to place me on the battlefield of Waterloo surpassed every historian's attempt to do the same. Hugo pointed out the many coincidences stacked up against Napoleon at Waterloo, and left the reader to contemplate the idea of natural justice, an idea I'd been toying with since discovering books and waking up to the many coincidences that led me to prison. I took note of how Hugo began and ended a chapter, how he created conflict, and how magnificently he resolved it. I'd flip back and forth, finding where a thought began, tracing its development, and studying its conclusion. While still in federal prison, I began teaching myself how to write, mostly by examining the styles of great authors who've stood the test of time. *Les Mis* placed Hugo at the top of that list. Everything he knew about writing was stuffed into its pages.

Everything he knew about life, too. Though two hundred years separated Victor Hugo from me, not much had changed with regard to human nature. His characters were remarkably real. I could relate to all of them, particularly, of course, protagonist Jean Valjean, the convict trying to make good on a lost life.

Like Valjean, I escaped from prison. I was no longer in a cell. I was in nineteenth-century Paris. I walked its streets, visited its abbeys, and waded knee-deep through its sewer system. In Nassau County Jail, we were locked up eighteen hours a day, and allowed to roam the tier block for the other six hours, with one hour of that time slotted for outdoor recreation. Cooped up for so long, cons normally race from their cells when the bars slide open. But I never left my cell, passing up that small dose of fake freedom for the real freedom *Les Mis* offered. Each night, I fell asleep with it on my chest. At dawn, I awoke to the little street urchin holding the broom; she swept away my depression. I didn't hear slamming bars, didn't feel cockroaches, or see any mice. I only heard, saw, and felt Hugo's characters and their emotions.

I didn't want the book to end. I stretched it out for as long as I could, about a month. Before placing it in the library's return bin, I flipped through the pages once more, stopping here and there to read a line, which brought to mind a section of the book that stayed with me. I wished Hugo had written a sequel, but some things are so perfect, they're better left alone.

About two years later, I was released from prison. I had served a total of eight and a half years. I had entered prison an aspiring gangster with ambition to rise in the Gambino Family. I returned home a book lover and writer.

Not long after my release, I was dating my future fiancée, a librarian and fellow bibliophile. We were browsing the shelves of a used book store, our favorite hobby, when I came across that familiar spine with the little street urchin. I grabbed the book, and hurried to the register. At home, I placed it on my shelf, like a trophy.

Naked Lunch

ELISSA SCHAPPELL

The first thing I noticed when I spotted my future husband, standing under the departures and arrivals board in Penn Station, was that he appeared to cut his own hair. The second, he was drinking a cup of coffee and reading a book. The third, the book was Francis Steegmuller's *Cocteau*.

I couldn't help but notice how the book's purple cover complimented his black turtleneck sweater and pants, safety orange socks, and high-tops. He looked like an artist (given the hair, a starving one). Was he, like Cocteau, an avant-garde filmmaker? A poet? An opium addict? Was that too much to hope for?

Or, I thought, my heart sinking, maybe the book was an accessory, purchased not because he was interested in the life of the artist but because the purple cover brought out the green in his eyes.

It seemed like kismet when I found us hip-to-hip in the mob moving down the steps to the Amtrak platform. When he turned and said, "This is hell, isn't it?" I swooned.

On the train he took the seat across the aisle from me, and put his book on the tray table. When he caught me trying to make out the image on the cover—two partially naked people of indeterminate gender emerging from a white paper canvas upon which Cocteau is painting—he asked, "You like Cocteau?"

"I do," I said. "What's not to like?"

I wished that instead of copies of *Spin* and *Vogue* I had a book of my own to flourish. I'd just finished Truman Capote's *Breakfast at Tiffany's*. Which was why I was on that train, bound for Washington, D.C. I hoped escaping New York City for the weekend would banish the case of mean reds I was suffering from, a result of a spirit-murdering job as the Junior Books Editor at an unglamorous women's magazine where I was sentenced to interminable hours of re-typing rejection letters, making copies, and tormenting co-workers by pretending to confuse the names of perennial magazine fave Leo Buscaglia, author of *Living, Loving and Learning*, and one of my high-school faves, Vincent Bugliosi, author of *Helter Skelter*. I'd also just stopped dating a man who nagged me about keeping my money in my shoe. Holly Golightly may have been damaged, selfish, and doomed to be alone, but at least she had a cat. And so I was off to D.C. to visit some friends, most notably an old flame.

Long story short: The train broke down. When my future husband asked me why I was going to D.C., I said to see a friend, which wasn't a lie exactly. When he asked what I did, I was more honest. I said I worked at a magazine, I read books and typed stories on letterhead so it appeared I was working.

"So, you're a writer," he said, clearly pleased. I blushed and mumbled about having no other wage-earning skills. He dismissed this.

"You write, so you're a writer."

He told me he'd dropped out of grad school a month before and come to New York with $150 in his pocket to pursue the literary life. (At twenty-two I thought this sounded romantic, not pretentious or phony.) He asked if I'd seen the movie *Brazil*. I hadn't. He saw it with a date, and was blown away. He'd said, "It's like Monty Python meets *1984*," to which the perplexed girl had replied, "Monty Who and what does the year 1984 have to do with anything?"

I laughed and rolled my eyes.

It took six hours to get to Baltimore, where he got off the train. I called my ex and told him I couldn't see him, that I'd met someone. He laughed. I didn't care. Not only had I met someone, he'd offered to lend me a book about Cocteau!

It was the first of many books he'd peddle during our courtship. There was J. G. Ballard's *Crash*, about a charismatic car-crash fetishist who, along with a cultish posse of car-crash victims, re-creates celebrity car accidents for sexual gratification (I figured he wanted to know straight away if I was like that *Brazil* girl); *The Complete Calvin and Hobbes* (I had no idea what this was supposed to signify. He's a clever six-year-old who has issues with authority and a rich fantasy life, and I am his giant stuffed tiger toy who only lives in his imagination? Was he possibly a furry? What the hell?); *Even Cowgirls Get the Blues* (Was he hinting at a thumb fetish? A fondness for girl-on-girl action? Did he hope I'd embrace some animal rights cause?); *On the Road*.

When I told him I'd never read it, he acted as though I'd confessed to not knowing the Pledge of Allegiance. Still, I wasn't a pure-blooded moron. I knew the Beats were bad boys. They dug jazz and drugs, treated women like shit, and inspired men to throw girlfriends into cars and drive like maniacs.

To wit: New Year's Eve, a Wednesday night, we drive down to Baltimore for a party. On the way we pick up Carlos, a photographer friend of my boyfriend's from high school. Somewhere between picking Carlos up and getting on the Expressway the two of them get the idea to blow off the party and see if we can't drive to San Francisco and back in time to go to work on Monday. I don't flatter myself to think that I really have a vote here. The moment the idea was born it became the plan. I sit in the back and write in my notebook. I'm not wearing socks.

The car quits outside of Aspen. It takes two days to get it fixed. Hopped up on truck-stop coffee and pecan milkshakes we have to haul ass for thirty-two straight hours to make it home, with an hour to shower and dress to make it to work on time. Sitting at my desk I feel my whole body buzzing, vibrating like the highway is still in my blood.

And then there was *Naked Lunch*.

That spring, six months after our fateful convergence in Penn Station, I moved from my three-girls-in-a-one-bedroom illegal sublet on the Upper East Side into the really crappy apartment on Staten Island he shared with three actors. On the walls of our eight-by-ten-foot room we spray-painted quotes from Hunter S. Thompson—*When the Going Gets Weird, the Weird Turn Pro*—and I painted daisies and a rocket ship. My books, including J. D. Salinger's *Nine Stories*, William Faulkner's *As I Lay Dying*, and, ironically, Virginia Woolf's *A Room of One's Own*, sit in a box by the bed. We've lately been talking about dropping out of New York, going to live out West for a while, so I haven't unpacked them. It's scary talk.

One night while we're sitting around our apartment with two of my boyfriend's friends, eating scrambled eggs and finishing off the gin, he puts on Laurie Anderson's *Mister Heartbreak*, which features William S. Burroughs doing a spoken-word piece called "Sharkey's Night." His voice, the edgy unnerving monotone of a morgue attendant you wouldn't want to leave alone with the body of your dead mother.

My boyfriend asks if I've read *Naked Lunch*.

"Of course I've *heard* of it," I say, acutely aware of the minute vibrations in the air caused by three sets of eyebrows being raised at once.

I remembered that *Naked Lunch* had been banned for being obscene, but mostly that Burroughs, while drunkenly attempting to shoot an apple off his wife's head, à la William Tell, had accidentally killed her.

"It will blow your mind," he says, oblivious to his unfortunate choice of words. "It's sooo far out there. You know, your classic hallucinatory cut-up novel."

"Classic, huh?"

"Visionary," he says. "A subversive masterpiece. The American underground wouldn't exist without Burroughs—"

"He from whom all blessings come . . . " one of his friends laughs. The three of them chuckle at their little in-joke. Come. *Cum.*

I grind my teeth.

While my boyfriend is in the kitchen getting more booze, the conversation turns to the candy scene in *Gravity's Rainbow*, another book I've never read but which must be just frickin' hilarious because those pretentious pricks are laughing their asses off. They're still not sure what the two of us living together means yet. I'm being hazed. Or maybe I'm being paranoid.

When he comes back with a jug-bottle of red wine and a copy of *Naked Lunch*, the Evergreen Black Cat first paperback edition published in 1966, the guys *ooh* and *ahh*.

The cover, which I imagine was once white, appears slightly jaundiced. The lurid red and violet type—two colors that have no business fraternizing—seems to pulsate. Inside, the pages are browning at the edges like the book has a disease, the kind no cream can cure. It was sinister looking. Beneath the title, a sunburst shaped like the seal of approval, declaring *With Massachusetts Supreme Court Decision and Excerpts from the Boston Trial*, and a blurb, from Norman Mailer: "The only American novelist living today who may conceivably be possessed by genius." I hadn't read Mailer yet either, but I knew *he'd* stabbed his wife.

"But it might not be your thing," my boyfriend says, taking his book back. "It's rough going at first. It might be a little too intense."

My face reddens.

"What's it about?" I ask.

His friends laugh in this world-weary-oh-you-poor-ridiculous-child sort of way.

"Good question," he says. "Ostensibly it's about this agent, William Lee—Burroughs's alter ego—a junkie and hustler who's on the run from the authorities, and looking for a fix. It bounces between Mexico, Tangiers, Freeland, this place called Interzone. . . . "

"Sounds like my cup of tea," I say. "*On the Road* on smack."

After our friends leave, and he's getting ready for bed, I pick it up. The book falls open naturally, like a Bible to the Psalms, and there in the middle is a twenty-year-old pull-out business reply postcard:

Do You Have What It Takes to Join the Underground? If you really know what the Underground is all about; if you're adult, literate and adventurous; then keep reading. Grove Press and Evergreen invite you to join the only club for people like you.

Subscribe to Evergreen book club for only $5 a month.

That's what he was asking me, wasn't it? *Do you have what it takes?* Before we bailed on New York, and moved across the country together, he wanted to be sure I did.

The next evening, while my boyfriend scrapes the dinner remnants into the trash, I start to read, trying to keep my expression neutral as I encounter the line "Dancing boys striptease with intestines, women stick severed genitals in their cunts, grind, bump, and flick it at the man of their choice. . . . " *Of course*, I think, *that's just the way we ladies roll.*

Crash had been appallingly graphic and stomach churning in parts. This, though. . . . It was how the ass-fucking, junk-addicted grandson of James Joyce would write. I could almost hear Burroughs cackling as he gleefully smashed the sewer pipes of the human condition with a hammer. I'd need psychic waders to slog through all the blood and jism and shit. But I would.

Occasionally, my boyfriend looks over at me while I'm reading like he's checking my temperature, waiting for me to put the book down or throw up in my mouth. I come close when I read "A coprophage calls for a plate, shits on it and eats the shit, exclaiming, 'Mmmm, that's my rich substance.'" Never again, I think, will I ever cook for this man. Indeed, I may never eat again. I do put the book down. I don't throw it across the room in terror the way I had Stephen King's *The Shining* when I was a girl, but I decide I'll read it only in the daylight, and outside the house. Because *Naked Lunch* is not a couch book—there's no curling up with Agent Lee, or Hassan. Nor is it a lull-you-into-sweet-dreamland book, despite the fact that someone is always *on the nod* or sleeping *the big sleep*. And it certainly isn't a book you dare take into the tub or engage in *any* state of nakedness. Although after reading some scenes, a Silkwood shower might be in order.

So I began reading *Naked Lunch* on the subway. Some of my fellow riders, innocent of the contents, studied the cover curiously, while others, not so innocent, flashed looks of worry and disgust in my direction. On one occasion, a gentleman clearly reading over my shoulder as he held onto the pole next to me waved his finger in my face and said, "Why are you reading that? You shouldn't read that."

It took me a moment to comprehend what he was saying. I was deep into the A.J.'s Party chapter, the "Blue Movies" section where three adolescents engaged in an orgy of pure sexual carnage take turns being hanged by the neck and fucked. If that wasn't party enough, there is an act of cannibalism, and finally a couple doused with gasoline immolating themselves. It ends with the players (for it *was* only a stag film) taking a bow.

Were I not trembling, struck mute, I'd have said to him, "It's satire—see, he calls the climax a *Deathgasm*. Burroughs intended that scene to protest the death penalty." If I'd had my wits about me, I'd have read him a line I think of to this day—"the sound like a stick broken in wet towels." Or fobbed the blame off on my boyfriend: "He gave it to me to read. I suspect he's testing me."

There were also times when a fan would catch my gaze, give me an almost imperceptible nod—*Password: Mugwump.* I knew that if I called out "Paging Dr. Benway" (the malignant doc who performs illegal abortions in the bathrooms of subway cars) they'd chuckle at our inside joke.

Naked Lunch had, as the Evergreen book club advertisement promised, made me feel like I was part of a community I never knew existed, made up of people who *got it, man.* . . . My boyfriend got it, his friends got it, and now I did, too.

When I told him I'd finished, he gave me a cryptic smile. "Well," he paused expectantly. "Well, what did you think?"

I made him wait a few seconds. "I can't describe it," I answered truthfully. "I feel like my atoms have been rearranged."

He nodded. He'd anticipated this.

"I really loved that line, *The old junky found a vein . . . blood blossoms in the dropper like—*"

He finished my sentence: "*a Chinese flower.*"

He smiled.

"Exactly."

The Story and Its Writer

ANTHONY DOERR

My parents' drafty two-story house in Ohio contains approximately forty-three gazillion books. At least one bookshelf stands in every room—hardcovers lined neatly along family room built-ins, rows of children's classics in the attic. Glossy art books squat on top of sofa tables; literary journals rest facedown on bathroom counters. Nightstands, toilet tanks, the pool table—everything is a bookshelf. An antique hutch in an upstairs bedroom comes particularly to mind, a piece of furniture so overloaded with my mother's ecology textbooks that it looks about to give out, as if to say: *C'mon. No more.*

Even the unfinished half of my parents' basement—concrete-floored, hairy with cobwebs, fringed with venerable toys and raccoon traps and dusty brewing supplies—carries books in its corners. And it was there, one afternoon when I was twenty-two, home from a year in Colorado working as a grill cook, that I stood in front of an old file cabinet surveying the titles stacked on top.

These were my brother's retired college books: Norton poetry anthologies; Joyce's *Portrait of the Artist as a Young Man*; *The Harper American Literature, Volume 2*. I was leaving for New Zealand in the morning, to live out of a backpack for seven months, and I had traveled overseas enough by then to know the importance of choosing the right book. The last thing you want is to find yourself five miles above the Pacific, fifteen hours left in your flight, with "Soaring, shivering, Candace inquiringly asked . . . " in your lap.

In the center of the stack a teal spine about three inches high drew my eye. The thickest of the lot. *The Story and Its Writer.*

I lifted the book down. Sixteen hundred onionskin pages, one hundred and fifteen short stories, three pounds. The stories were arranged alphabetically by their writers: Chinua Achebe to Richard Wright. Such a book would be absurd for backpacking.

And yet, as I held it, the book slipped open to an early page as if under its own power. I read, "Upon the half decayed veranda of a small frame house that stood near the edge of a ravine near the town of Winesburg, Ohio, a fat little old man walked nervously up and down."

Sherwood Anderson. One sentence. It was enough. I lugged the book upstairs and wedged it into my carry-on.

I landed in Auckland and boarded a ferry and decided to hike the circumference of Great Barrier Island, a remote, windswept protuberance of bays and hills in the Hauraki Gulf. I bought potatoes, four sleeves of Chips Ahoy!, a can of tuna, two pounds of noodles, and a can with a picture of a tomato on it that said *Tomato Sauce*. I bought white kitchen trash bags: one to keep my sleeping bag dry, another inside which to sheath the three-pound brick of *The Story and Its Writer*.

For my first seventy-two hours on that island it rained every minute. On my third night—I hadn't seen another human being in two days—a storm came in and my tent started thrashing about as if large men had ahold of each corner and were trying to shred it. Sheep were groaning nearby, and my sleeping bag was flooding, and I wanted to go home.

I leaned into the little shuddering tent vestibule and got my stove lit. I started boiling noodles. I carefully cut open my can of tomato sauce, anticipating spaghetti. I dipped my finger in. It was ketchup.

I almost started crying. Instead I switched on my flashlight and opened *The Story and Its Writer.* For no reason I could articulate, I began with "Walker Brothers Cowboy," by Alice Munro.

By the second paragraph the tent had disappeared. The storm had disappeared. I had disappeared. I had become a little girl, my father was a salesman for Walker Brothers, and we were driving through the Canadian night, little bottles in crates clinking softly in the backseat.

Next I flipped to Italo Calvino's "The Distance of the Moon." Now I was clambering up a ladder onto the moon. The last page left me smiling and awed and misty: "I imagine I can see her, her or something of her, but only her, in a hundred, a thousand different vistas, she who makes the Moon the Moon. . . . "

Then I lost myself in the menacing, half-drunk suburbia of Raymond Carver. Then Isak Dinesen's "The Blue Jar." The line "When I am dead you will cut out my heart and lay it in the blue jar" is still underlined—underlined by a younger, wetter, braver version of me—as I sit here in Idaho with the book almost twenty years later, warm and dry, no ketchup in sight. I press my nose to the page: I smell paper, mud, memory.

When I eventually stopped reading that night, and washed back into myself, I had eaten two entire sleeves of Chips Ahoy. The rain had stopped. I unzipped the tent door and stepped back onto Great Barrier Island. The stars were violently bright, electric-blue. The Milky Way was stretched south to north. Orion was upside down.

For seven months I carried *The Story and Its Writer* through New Zealand. I hiked my way from the tip of the North Island to the bottom of the South Island and Nadine Gordimer came with me; Flannery O'Connor came with me; Tim O'Brien came with me. On a sheep farm in Timaru, John Steinbeck whispered, "The high grey-flannel fog of winter closed off the Salinas Valley from the sky and from all the rest of the world." In a hostel in Queenstown, Joyce whispered, "His soul swooned slowly as he heard the snow falling faintly through the universe." In a climber's hut beneath the summit of Mount Tongariro, John Cheever whispered, "Is forgetfulness some part of the mysteriousness of life?"

Maybe we build the stories we love into ourselves. Maybe we *digest* stories. When we eat a pork chop, we break up its cellular constituents, its proteins, its fats, and we absorb as much of the meat as we can into our bodies. We become part pig. Eat an artichoke, become part artichoke. Maybe the same thing is true for what we read. Our eyes walk tightropes of sentences, our minds assemble images and sensations, our hearts find connections with other hearts. A good book becomes part of who we are, perhaps as significant a part of us as our memories. A good book flashes around inside, endlessly reflecting. Its shapes, its people, its places become our shapes, our people, our places.

We take in a story. We metabolize it. We *incorporate* it.

Imagine you could draw a map of all the experiences you've had in your life, and superimpose it over a map of all the books you've read in your life. Here you worried your daughter was failing out of school, here you gave a nun a stick of chewing gum, here you saw a man dressed as a referee weeping in a Honda Accord. And here a boy in an egg-blue suit handed you an ornate invitation to a party at Jay Gatsby's, here you met the harpooner Queequeg at the Spouter Inn, here you floated a stretch of the Mississippi with a slave named Jim. Here you crouched in a tent in the rain and read Isak Dinesen's "The Blue Jar" for the very first time.

Everything would be intertwined; everything would transubstantiate. There would be your life, your memories, your loves and doubts. Then there would be the faint tracery of the lives of your parents, your grandparents, their parents. Then there would be your dreams. And then there would be all the books you have ever read.

I spilled hot chocolate on *The Story and Its Writer*. I dropped a corner of it in a river. I brought it back across the Pacific and went to graduate school and used it to write literature essays and then to fumble through my first efforts as a teacher. And now I have my own house, my own dozen bookshelves, and the big teal spine of *The Story and Its Writer* sits on one behind my desk as if waiting to fall open again. If I look at it long enough it seems to pulse.

We are all mapmakers: We embed our memories everywhere, inscribing a private and intensely complicated latticework across the landscape. We plant root structures of smells and textures in the apartments of lovers and the station wagons of friends and in the backyards of our parents. But we are readers, too. And through stories we manage to live in multiple places, lead multiple lives. Through stories we rehearse empathy; through stories we live the emotional lives of other people—people in the future, people in the sixteenth century, people living in Pakistan right now. We fall, we drift, we lose ourselves in other selves.

What I have learned and relearned all my life, what I learned growing up in a house overspilling with books, what *The Story and Its Writer* taught me, what I relearned last night reading *Harry Potter* to my five-year-old sons, is that if you are willing to let yourself go, to fall into the dazzle of well-made sentences, each strung lightly one after the next—"Upon the half decayed veranda of a small frame house that stood near the edge of a ravine near the town of Winesburg, Ohio, a fat little old man walked nervously up and down."—if you live with stories, you will never be alone.

Invisible Man

DAVID HAJDU

A narrow alcove runs from the sidewalk to the basement entrance of an apartment house on the north side of West 4th
Street, about half a block from West 12th Street in Greenwich
Village—a notoriously implausible intersection that betrays the
streets' provenance as cow paths in the neighborhood's prehistory
as farmland. When I was an undergraduate at New York University, in the late 1970s, an enterprising old Villager used this bubble
of found public space during the evening hours to run a makeshift
bookstore. Thinking back more than thirty years later, I realize I
may be wrong about the proprietor's age. If he was thirty-five then,
he was elderly to me, and I conceived of him romantically as a
crusty bohemian mysterioso, the Joe Gould of bookselling. I never
learned his name. My friends and I in the would-be literati of
NYU called him "the book hustler," in admiration, and several of
us spent a fair amount of time browsing through the crates to
study his small but always interestingly and miraculously ever-
replenishing stock, on our way to the 12th Street Bar.

Once, I came by as he was setting up shop, and offered some
help, dragging boxes and hoisting them into position as book
stacks. Established now as an insider, I pitched in on a few more
occasions and was eventually entrusted with the task of assisting
in the preparation of fresh merchandise for sale. I could tell from

the "Used" stickers on the new arrivals' spines that they had come from the NYU bookstore or its trashbins. Flipping through one volume after another, the book hustler checked each of them to see if it had been written on or marked with a highlighter. If he found only a few notes in pencil, he tried to erase them. If he found lots of markings, he put the book in a pile to be displayed near the sidewalk. If he found nothing but clean pages, he handed the book to me, and it was my job to peel the "Used" sticker off.

I know better than to read too much into the merchandising technique of an itinerant Village eccentric who was, as I saw him in my youth, and who remains, in the only way I can recall him, a walking cliché. Still . . . I've thought more than once over the years about the way he categorized—or tried to pass off—books that had been read but not written in as unused, and it strikes me still as worth consideration. After all, to read is to absorb, to take in, to internalize the work of a writer; it is to be a partner in something profoundly intimate—the exchange of thoughts from one mind to another. But to pick up a pen or a pencil and scrawl onto the pages of a book, to write back to a piece of writing, is something different and perhaps something more. It represents not merely passive absorption of the content but active response to it—the intimacy between writer and reader made physical. A book written in is a book employed, taken up as a tool, utilized. It calls for a sticker that marks it as *used*.

Being a lifelong buyer of secondhand books, I have owned countless titles marked up by previous owners—including some previously marked by countless owners; and, being a reader rather than a collector, I have passed on or resold a great many of them to be marked again. For years, I browsed the used stacks carefully and tried to avoid getting copies that were heavily inked up. Now, when I want a book, I tend to click lazily to eBay or Amazon, where information on the interior pages of used books is typically scant or wildly, almost poetically, cryptic. When the package containing an old book I've purchased through the Web arrives in the mail, I know the pages may hold wondrous surprises. Not long ago, I bought a used paperback copy of *Under the Sign of Saturn*, a collection of essays by Susan Sontag, through Amazon, and the book came with nearly every paragraph underlined. As I read the text, I grew inured to the ink lines; I became fascinated, though, by the few passages unmarked. On page 194 of the chapter on Elias Canetti, for example, the first two lines of the second paragraph are the only sentences not underlined on that page: "Canetti refuses the victim's part. There is much chivalry in his portrait of his mother." Why, why, I have to wonder, would anyone find that specifically unworthy of note? Was the reader so versed in Canetti that Sontag's comments seemed perfunctory? Did he or she have a mother problem? If so, I don't exactly care, though I can't help but want to know.

Of all the books with past-owner's markings that I've ever had, the one that has compelled me most is a paperback of Ralph Ellison's *Invisible Man*, which I bought from the West 4th Street book hustler when I was in college. I still have it. The novel itself has been a favorite of mine since I first read that copy, and the spectral presence of an unknown other reader—one revealable only through inference and visible only through the imagination—has always, in my mind, been inextricable from the dreamscape of elusive identity that Ellison conjured in his mesmeric prose.

My book is a trade paperback published by Vintage in 1972, just a few years before I bought it. Originally priced at $1.95, it cost me a quarter. The book had at least one previous owner, a reader who neatly—exceedingly neatly—underlined a paragraph here, a lone sentence there, and sometimes a passage of a page and a half or so in length. Fastidiously, though in a light hand, the person drew nearly every underline with a tool of some sort—a ruler or, I suspected by the way the ink sometimes bled on the bottom of the lines, the side of a notecard. The fact that Ellison himself was well known to be a neatnik led me, fleetingly, to fantasize that the book had been his own. Such is the sort of preposterousness I found myself entertaining in the absence of actual information to identify someone I felt I had begun to know through the feeling of reading through his or her eyes.

Who was this person, this third mind poked between Ellison's and mine? He was invisible, yes—but a man or a woman? Black like Ellison or white like me? My predecessor to the book's pages underlined what adds up to more than a thousand words of text from the bravura oration by Rev. Barbee, Ellison's answer to Father Mapple's sermon in *Moby-Dick*. On page 129, the line "Black, black, black!" is underscored firmly, and so, earlier in the same section, are these sentences: "Some say he was a Greek. Some a Mongolian. Others a mulatto—and others still, a simple white man of God." Fittingly, for *Invisible Man*, I could only guess what the evidence was inadequate to reveal, and my speculation is useful only in pointing to the limitations—no, the simplemindedness—of my method.

I tried teasing meaning from the very ink, which was a shade of green. Who uses a green pen, I wondered? An architect or an illustrator? And what would that tell me? That architects read fiction? My worldview was expanding. In time, I realized that the ink might have been blue originally and faded to green. But what of that fact? Had the last owner read the book on the beach and left it in the sun? None of this added up to suggest anything other than the possibility that the book has been owned by a Greek-Mongolian-mulatto architect on vacation.

After college, when I started working in my first job in publishing—as a junior writer for a trade journal—I learned about "non-repros," special pens used in those days to mark up galleys for publication. The ink was dark enough to be read by the production staff but light enough not to reproduce in the printing process. This ink, which made invisibility literal, was almost exactly the color of the pen lines in my copy of *Invisible Man*. Hence, I deduced that my mystery reader may have been a professional editor, and that proposition led me back to the text in search of clues to the workings of the editorial mind. In them, I hoped to find ways to reduce the number of rejection letters I was getting for the stories I was writing when I got home from my trade-journal job.

My nameless forerunner to the pages of *Invisible Man* did reveal himself in one way that opened up the book to me. He or she was acutely attuned to the lyricism of Ellison's language. Most of the underlines—and the small handful of scribbles and notations in the margins—indicate passages of special beauty. On page 34: "On up the road, past the buildings, with the southern verandas half-a-city-block long, to the sudden forking, barren of building, birds, or grass, where the road turned off to the insane asylum." And on page 226, with a little five-point star drawn next to the type: "I was sitting in a cold, white rigid chair and a man was looking at me out of a bright third eye that glowed from the center of his forehead." Ellison, who began his career writing for organs of the Far Left such as *The New Masses*, was a political writer, and *Invisible Man* veered at points toward the polemical. But I read the book with its poetry underscored.

While I was an undergraduate at NYU, Ellison was teaching at the school—one class a term, a literature seminar. I mistakenly thought the course was restricted to graduate students, and never signed up for it. In my last term, I learned from a professor I thought of as a mentor, the playwright Tad Mosel, that I was wrong (about Ellison's course and many other things). Mosel put in a call to Ellison, and he agreed to meet me in his university office. I have subsequently read in Arnold Rampersad's fine biography of Ellison that he had elegantly appointed quarters, and an assistant, at One Fifth Avenue, off Washington Square. That's not where I met him; I saw him—briefly, twice—in a smallish, grayish space in the English Department. Ellison was gracious, courtly, and impeccably groomed. I think I stared at his perfect, rakish little mustache. I was panicked in his company and no doubt overcompensated by over-talking. When he got a chance, Ellison told me a sweet allegorical story about a poor man he had watched pulling the newspaper out of a trashbin. He told me I should think of that anonymous garbage-picker as my imagined model reader. I no longer recall how I responded. I remember only having no idea what he was talking about.

Several years later, I read Ellison's autobiographical essay, "The Little Man at Chehaw Station," and I recognized that he had offered me a variation on the theme of the piece, a dramatic argument against naive presumption. As ever, Ellison was thinking about the elusiveness of identity; and, as always, he saw both tyranny and grace in anonymity.

I visited Ellison only a couple of times and could not fairly say I knew him. (After his death, I was one of several writers invited to read from his work at the groundbreaking ceremony for the memorial constructed in his honor at Riverside Park, and I was surprised to have been asked.) As a fan of his, rather than a protégé or even a student, I wanted during our tentative acquaintance to ask him for his autograph. I brought my copy of *Invisible Man* with me when I saw him, but I could never muster the wherewithal to ask him to sign it. Embarrassed to own a secondhand paperback, I was probably reluctant to ask him to inscribe a book that someone else had written all over. What if he saw all those green-pen markings and read one of the underlined passages? Wouldn't he wonder, exactly as I did, *what person would do such a thing?*

Roar and More

JULIA GLASS

For Karla Kuskin

I was not a child for whom books are rare and precious objects, for whom the public library is a temple on a hill, a sacred lode of strange and glorious treasure. Don't get me wrong: My town library was a favorite haunt, but in the homes where I grew up—from my parents' first, snug apartment near Harvard Square to the house in a pastoral suburb where they would settle for good when I was nine—books were beyond numerous; they were downright invasive, filling bookcases in nearly every room and cartons stashed everywhere else. My mother worried that the beams supporting the attic would buckle, leading to the collapse of our modest house, which was built for a farmhand, not a bibliophile. Her anxieties fell on stubborn, well-educated ears. For my father, a scholar of Meso-American archaeology, reading was akin to breathing. The very objects of his scrutiny were books: He specialized in the study of pre-Columbian hieroglyphic manuscripts, the primitive yet vividly illustrated work of Central American indigenous peoples (Mixtecs, Zapotecs, Aztecs).

In a baby picture staged and produced by Dad, my infant self lies naked on the changing table, belly down, propped on chubby elbows, gazing at the pages of an antique tome in an obscure foreign language. That picture never ceases to amuse us all. Some of my happiest early memories—from around age five—are those in which I keep my father company while he works in his study. He's at his desk, reading or typing; I sit cross-legged on the floor, beside a wall of bookshelves, pulling out volumes and browsing at random. The ones I remember best featured strikingly grue-some images of bloody rites, from the Sun Dance of the Sioux to the evisceration of enemy warriors by Aztec priests. Chilling, yes, but I delighted in doing what my father did, poring over the bizarre yet fascinating customs of people who lived (reassur-ingly) far from us in time as well as place.

But here is a more singular memory from that era: My parents and I are staying in a hotel room—so rare an occasion that I imagine we must have been en route to or from a visit with my father's ancient, elegant grandmother in Corsicana, Texas. (We went everywhere by car.) I am sitting on the rug, leaning against the foot of the bed, watching *Captain Kangaroo* on TV.

I was a fairly monogamous watcher of children's TV circa 1959; for me, the Captain was It. I did not care for the simpering hostess of *Romper Room*; Bozo the Clown was diverting but shal-low. (The philosophizing of Fred Rogers and the shaggy shenani-gans of *Sesame Street* came along much later, by which time I was thrilled to be in school, silliness a babyish thing of the past.)

I loved Mr. Green Jeans, the cartoons (Mighty Manfred and Mr. Magoo), the Danny Kaye soundtrack to the puppet shows, the goofball (and ping-pong ball) antics; but when the Captain sat in his reading chair and pulled out a book—usually a book he'd read before, many times—I was in the heaven I knew best. Endlessly revisiting the same favorite stories is a luxury crucial to any decent childhood. And so, again and again, he'd read *Mike Mulligan and His Steam Shovel*, *Make Way for Ducklings*, *Curious George*, *Stone Soup*, and *Caps for Sale*, because he knew that we, his audience, couldn't get enough of them. (I've wondered, read-ing these books to my children forty years later, whether they

owe their classic status largely to the Captain. Surely, to any author of picture books, Captain Kangaroo was yesteryear's
Oprah.)

Now and then, however, he'd introduce a brand-new book.
That morning, as I sat in that hotel room, he read a book called
Roar and More. You could describe it as a book of short, clever
animal poems and you wouldn't be wrong, but such a description
would miss entirely what made this book so different, so deliciously quirky.

The animals in *Roar and More* are the usual nursery suspects:
lion, elephant, tiger, snake, kangaroo, fish, cat, dog (a gregarious
band of mongrels), a bee, a mouse, and a giraffe with a mighty
loooooooong neck. They are plainly yet appealingly drawn, in an
artsy coloring-book style: calligraphic outlines filled with flat
shades of yellow, gray, and toothpaste green. The doggerel is
sweet, funny, and wry, though it's no match for the gymnastic
wordplay of Seuss, the bow-tied wit of Ciardi or Nash, the
wickedness of Silverstein. There's a touch of folk wisdom in its
contemplation of fish and giraffes, and the poet's musings on alternative uses for an elephant's trunk should lead any child to
dream up several more.

The true charm and surprise of this book, however, lie in the
punch lines to its poems: Turn the page after each one and you
come upon a spread that makes a verbal pictogram of the special
noise made by each animal, spelled out in a typeface and font
size suited exactly to the personality and **VOLUME** of that
noise: with or sans serif, **bold** or *italic*, FILLING THE WHITE
VOID or timidly skirting the margins. These pages are the splen-
did soul of the book—a source of versatile joy to reader and lis-
tener alike (and, not insignificantly, catnip to any parent who
ever longed to be onstage). The roar of the lion is, typographi-
cally speaking, a monument to its virility; the snarl of the tiger
is ferocity restrained. The "fuzzing sort of buzz" made by the

solitary bee etches on the page a terse, zipperlike pattern, while the dogs perform a visual brawl, a riff of *rowf*s and *yarf*s and *yip*s and *yap*s. Fish? A ballet of zeroes as bubbles. Kangaroos? Imagine their percussive impact on Australia's hard-packed earth. The giraffe . . . ah, well, that's the punch line to top all the others.

The foregoing appreciation was crafted, of course, by me the grown-up writer and dissector-of-the-world, the seasoned parent who's read a zillion picture books (some of them a zillion times), the looker-back on a childhood that led me logically—if not in the straightest of lines—toward the extraordinary fortune of making a living at something I really love to do: writing stories of my own.

But rewind to that hotel room, somewhere (perhaps) on a long drive between Boston and Texas. Here's where I wish I could remember hearing Captain Kangaroo read this book aloud. I don't, not a bit. But what I do remember is falling in love with that book, based on that one reading, and asking my parents, right then, to buy it for me. I wanted to own it. This was the first time I wanted to claim a book I'd discovered on my own (okay, with an assist from the Captain). I wanted to be able to hold it, page through it, ask to have it read to me, at will. In short order, thanks to parents who understood that books are a staple of life, I did. And it felt somehow magic, to hold in my hands this book I'd seen only on TV, in the hands of Captain Kangaroo.

How long it held favored status over my many other books, I can't begin to recall. But I do know that I made sure it was never bequeathed to another child—not even my little sister—as so many other books were. Nor was it ever relegated to the cartons of books I've had to banish to storage at various junctures of my life. (Half a dozen such boxes that fell into limbo after my divorce, twenty years ago, still sit in a corner of my parents' barn. The books in those boxes do not deserve this fate, but I feel too guilty to face what I suspect will be damage by mice and mildew.)

When I left for college, I took along such essential books as a dictionary, a thesaurus, and my high school yearbook, but I also chose an armful of beloved books as talismans of home, reminders of the me I thought I was leaving behind for good. They included the Narnia books, a septet of brittle paperbacks I'd ordered from the U.K. in third grade (because these were the ones owned by my worldly teacher and I liked the jacket art better than that of the American editions); an Oxford anthology of poetry for which I'd saved up babysitting money in junior high; my favorite Edward Gorey (*Three Ladies Beside the Sea*); a coffee-table book on Pre-Raphaelite painting; a collection of Grimm's fairy tales; a Dover paperback of signs and symbols; and *Roar and More*. These books—which gathered a few oddball companions—followed me through my four years at Yale, on campus and off, then returned to my childhood bedroom while I spent a year living in Paris, pursuing my ambitions as an artist. But once I returned to the States, setting up house as a painter in Brooklyn, *Roar and More* was front and center among the books I took to furnish a life on my own.

I doubt that I opened this book for the next fifteen years, though it moved with me from Brooklyn to Manhattan to Hoboken, then back across the river to Manhattan. Its pages grew quietly yellow (though they did not crumble); its black spine faded in the sun. Its dust jacket—if it ever had one—was long gone. I'm sure the first time I opened it in nearly two decades would have been in early 1996, just after my first son, Alec, was born. I started reading to him at once, and the first books I read were "firsts" of my own, the few I'd saved from my earliest years. I would sit cross-legged on the floor beside a bookcase, nestle Alec in the well of my lap, pull down book after book, and read. His eyes would wander, his hands knit the air; I'd read until he began to complain or hint that he'd rather be eating. I could have read him anything—the novels I was reading to myself, articles from the latest *New Yorker*, album notes to the jazz LPs treasured by his father (the father who'd wanted to name him Thelonious)— but I suppose I was channeling the Captain.

Alec grew quickly into loving books—though not, I might add, into loving jazz. (Aesthetic nurture is not a slam-dunk proposition.) In our small one-bedroom apartment, we'd made a tiny room for him by walling off a corner of the living room with (what else?) bookshelves. The floor of this nook was often a slippery sea of books. Because the children's room of our branch library was governed by a graduate of the Almira Gulch Finishing School, a woman who made the place inhospitable to the very readers it was meant to serve, I spent absurd sums of money to provide Alec with a library of his own. And I let him have his way with his books; sometimes he fell asleep among or on top of them, pages bent or wet with drool, spines split, jackets torn in two. (One day he removed all the jackets and asked me to throw them away because they were a nuisance. Instead, I tucked them in a large manila envelope—lost now somewhere in my attic.)

Roar and More, however, was one of three or four picture books I still kept sequestered with mine. I would read it, often, on request, but I could not bear to see it mauled or torn. Early on, I'd tried to buy Alec a copy for himself—only to discover, at my local bookseller, that it was out of print. I was incredulous; how could such a great book be *out of print*? I remember raising my voice in the bookstore, alarming the young woman who'd told me this outrageous news.

What idiot publisher had abandoned this book? Had some fool declared it out of date or style? My son adored it as much as I had. On his fourth birthday, I used a fat Sharpie to copy the jacket illustration of a crouching, roaring lion, enlarging the image to fill a sheet of paper five feet square, then cut out paper **roar**s, in speech bubbles, so that Alec's birthday guests could play Pin the Roar on the Lion.

Just as Alec began to grow beyond picture books, his brother, Oliver, was born. Once again, I went through the blissful ritual of reading to a captive infant—though I had far less time than I'd had after Alec was born. Like Alec, Oliver loved *Roar and More*. Again and again, happily, theatrically, I read it—roaring, snarling, honking, barking, buzzing.

About this time, I began work on my second novel, *The Whole World Over*. In part, it's about the demands and compromises of being a parent. I found that as I portrayed the relationship between my fictional mother and her small son, the books they shared were essential to their ongoing conversation. At first reflexively, and then with a willful and pleasant self-indulgence, I wove throughout the novel several books that my sons and I had shared—some from my own childhood, others exclusively from theirs.

Gradually, children's books crept into other relationships in the novel as well. An older man, when he finds out that he will become a grandfather, unpacks the boxes of his children's belongings that his late wife had stored away. Among the books, he finds (how could I resist?) a copy of *Roar and More*. To his grown niece, who's with him when he makes this discovery, he reads aloud the poem about fish and the unassuming lives they lead.

I knew I would have to seek permission to borrow this poem—and probably pay for that permission. I did not want to leave it out; to me, this scene captured an important transition in the older man's life, an impromptu return to his life as a much younger father yet also a passing of the father's mantle to his son. Children's books, when passed from one generation to the next, evoke as much longing for the past, as much awareness of mortality, as any heirloom possibly can. I wanted the lightness of the poem to offset the weight of the moment.

My editor's assistant, Millicent, diligently tracked down permissions for nearly a dozen quotations I refused to surrender for expediency's sake: an Emily Dickinson verse, a lyric from the musical *Camelot*, short (and sometimes costly) passages from Dr. Seuss, Margaret Wise Brown, and authors far less famous. A few weeks before my book was set to go to press, all these permissions had been secured except for the lines from *Roar and More*. The poet—the author *and* illustrator of the book—was Karla Kuskin. Millicent had sent several communications to the publisher that controlled the rights to most of her books, but they had gone unanswered.

"Most of her books"? I pondered this aside. Suddenly, a rather obvious, stunningly stupid question occurred to me: Who was this Karla Kuskin, other than a name in small print beneath the title of the book I'd owned longer than any other? I'd had this book for so long that I didn't really think of it as having an *author*. This may sound disingenuous, but here's the thing: When you are a small child besotted with books, the books themselves—especially the ones you love best—are autonomous things, concrete yet abstract, like the stuffed animals and building blocks that help you travel to places where only *you* can go. At bedtime, you don't ask your mom, "Read me some E. B. White." You ask for Stuart Little, or Charlotte and Wilbur. You ask for a fairy tale or a dog story; for Pippi, Babar, or—nowadays— Toot and Puddle. Your favorite characters—you know *them*. From a mile away, you could spot the Man in the Yellow Hat, Mrs. Mallard, Olivia, or Ferdinand the bull; but H. A. Rey, Robert McCloskey, Ian Falconer, and Munro Leaf—who the heck are they? Authorial celebrity is sabotaged yet further when picture books lose their jackets, because when they do—whether by accident or, as in our home, by decree—they shed their authors' biographies as well. Many prolific children's writers are also prone to changing dance partners—that is, illustrators—making their books even harder to see as distinctly their own. (Dr. Seuss may be the exception to this rule. Children become aware of him as a uniquely creative individual, perhaps because they hear their parents call the guy a "genius." He's the Bob Dylan of children's authors, too eccentrically, definitively . . . well, *Seussian* . . . to be confused with anyone else.)

But there I was, forty-nine years old, an author myself, never having stopped to contemplate the identity, the personal story, of the woman who created a book so important to me for so long— or to hunt down any others she might have written.

When I began to focus on Karla Kuskin, just her name, the first thing I realized was that I'd seen it on at least one other book we owned. I went into my sons' room (both boys now shared our apartment's one true bedroom) and scanned the shelves. Good lord: A book they both loved, one that had been recommended by a fellow mother, that I'd relished reading countless times, was *The Philharmonic Gets Dressed*—written by Karla Kuskin, illustrated (perfectly) by Simont. (I could write an entire essay on that book, too. I will say just two things. One, if you have a small child who loves music, or who loves to giggle over underwear, or both, this is your book. Two, if by chance you have recently left behind a much-loved life in New York City, possibly in exchange for a beautiful seaside town in Massachusetts, and even if you have few regrets, this book will put a big fat nostalgic lump in your throat.)

Needless to say, *Philharmonic* was naked—no jacket, no author bio—yet listed on the back were twelve books "Also by Karla Kuskin," all with evocative titles such as *Any Me I Want to Be* and *James and the Rain* and *Which Horse Is William?* The list did not, however, include *Roar and More*. Since I knew my beloved book was out of print, I could only wonder if other books she'd written had also fallen off the shelves; what I knew for certain was that I'd spent a lifetime missing volumes of this woman's poetry and wit, both verbal and visual. Whenever a new book by one of your favorite "adult" writers is published, you know it—from reviews and ads in the paper, perhaps from its prominence in your bookstore window—but rare is the "juvenile" author whose latest opus gets much fanfare. (The exceptions to this rule we know all too well.)

Millicent persisted valiantly on the permissions front. If we could not find out how or where to get permission to reprint the fish verse from *Roar and More*, I'd have to delete it from *The Whole World Over*. Finally, at the proverbially penultimate hour, Millicent discovered that the rights to *Roar and More* were, uniquely, in the hands of a literary agent who happened to be Kuskin's nephew. She approached him with the kind of understated desperation one must devise when one doesn't want the imploree to realize that he or she may ask for the moon because one is, quite simply, up against a wall.

The nephew got back to us just in time, and the price he named for use of the poem was curious. He asked for two things. First, he knew that my publisher, Pantheon, was a hotbed of graphic fiction; might he secure a box of graphic novels for himself? (No sooner asked than granted.) Second, when my novel was published, would I send him a copy personally inscribed to his aunt?

Of course I would. But wait. I was speechless. Hadn't the Captain read *Roar and More*, clearly the work of a mature author, back in the 1950s? I had seen Captain Kangaroo's obituary two years before, and, not to be rude, but surely Karla Kuskin was also . . . no longer with us.

Had I not been so Web-challenged at the time, I would already have done what I did next: Google Karla Kuskin. In fact, I'm pretty sure this was the first time I ever "visited" Wikipedia. I discovered not only that she was alive and well, living right there in New York City, but that *Roar and More* had been the very first of more than sixty books she'd thus far written and/or illustrated.

Karla Kuskin was born in 1932 and, like me, she had gone to Yale College and majored in studio art—with an obvious affinity for words as well. *Roar and More* was her 1955 BFA thesis in graphic design. She published it as a book in 1956, the year I was born.

Fifty years later, in 2006, my novel *The Whole World Over* came out. Halfway through the book, my character Saga, a young woman disabled by an accident, sits with her elderly Uncle Marsden on a couch in the large house they share. He pages through a copy of *Roar and More* that he's just unearthed from a box of his son Michael's childhood belongings, a box packed away by Michael's late mother. Now Michael and his wife are expecting the twins who will make the older man a grandfather. The niece and the uncle laugh together over the silly poems he reads aloud for the first time in decades.

Saga looked closely at the illustration of pastel green fish. She felt a gust of cold air from an open window. She was sure she could remember Uncle Marsden reading this book to her, this very verse, along with her cousins. He paged slowly to the end—past a cat, a pack of yellow dogs, bees, a mouse, a giraffe—and closed the book. He let it sit on his lap, both hands flat on the cover. Saga noticed all the brown spots on his hands, the sliver of fragile white skin under the edge of his wedding ring.

I inscribed a copy of the book to Karla Kuskin and marked for her the page on which this scene occurs. I don't remember my inscription, but I'm sure I gushed. I paper-clipped to the jacket a mash note in which I told her about my lifelong love of her first book—which was, in a different sense, my first book as well. As instructed, I sent my novel and my note to Kuskin's nephew.

About a month later, I received an elegantly addressed envelope at my house, the sender Karla Kuskin on Joralemon Street in Brooklyn (an address no more than ten blocks from the apartment where I lived and worked for my first six years in New York, first as a painter and then, by the time I moved, as a writer). The note inside the envelope, written on three sheets of flowered stationery, hand-colored in an offhand way, begins: *Dear Julie, I once read that "you do not have to thank someone for thanking you," that was Emily Post who said so, and I will disregard it if I have a good enough reason to; you and your card are my reason.*

She commented on details of my fan letter, my stories about *her* stories. She told me that she was reading my novel and finding it (thus far) "very delicious." She closed with the word *thanks* underscored three times; beside her signature, she penned a girlish heart and shaded it in with red pencil. The me who read that letter (at least the first few times) was four or five years old, the me I thought I'd left behind for good when I left home for college.

I contemplated writing Karla Kuskin to thank her for thanking me for thanking her—take that, Emily Post!—but decided I'd let the circle complete itself there. She hadn't asked me any questions or suggested that we meet; I didn't want to seem pushy. Nor did I live in New York anymore—though I made it back a few times a year. Sooner or later, I thought, I'd find a good excuse to write once more and offer to take Ms. Kuskin out for lunch. I'd bring along *Roar and More* and ask her to inscribe it to me. I was glad to know exactly where to find her—I knew her block, her subway stop—and I no longer needed the nephew to act as a go-between.

Nearly four years later—two weeks ago—I embarked on writing this essay. As I did so, I decided that the time had come to write Karla Kuskin again; I'd invite her out for lunch on my next city visit, tell her about the essay, and promise her a copy of the finished book (this one). I was most of the way through a draft of the essay, a few days ago now, when I decided to refresh my memory about the details of her Yale degree and her bibliography. I went straight to Wikipedia and typed her name in the search field. When her page popped up, my eyes immediately took in something different and profoundly upsetting. After her name, her birth date was followed by the date of her death: August 20, 2009. She died seven months ago today, at age seventy-seven, of a rare disease called corticobasal degeneration. I followed the link to her obituary in the *New York Times*—a long one, quoting two of her poems. At the end of her life, she lived in Seattle, not New York.

My *Roar and More* sits beside me now, on my kitchen table in Massachusetts. It's soiled, nicked, tarnished with fingerprints. Here and there, the pages bear oxidized stains, sepia droplets and smears. On the cover, somebody couldn't resist coloring, with brown crayon, both O's in the title. Inside, on the front endpaper, that somebody's name floats mid-page in blue ballpoint pen, the letters irregular in size and placement:

J U Li E

I had barely learned to write my name when I claimed the book as *mine*.

For the first time, I wonder which parent walked into what store and bought it for me. Sad to say, I retain only the wispiest memory of my father, a man with a sly wit and a talent for animal mimicry, reading *Roar and More* aloud. At eighty-one, he's still sharp, still funny, still the scholar surrounded by his books, but emphysema has robbed him of breath, so he no longer reads to my sons. On mild days, however, he sits on his front deck and holds up his side of a dialogue with songbirds in the surrounding trees.

I find it fascinating that my strongest, earliest memory attached to this book is of how I acquired it. I am not a "collector" of books, so I can count on one hand those for which the acquisition looms larger than the book itself. I still own my childhood copies of *Goodnight Moon* and *The Cat in the Hat*; I even own a book, *The Story of Ping*, that my mother owned when she was a child. But I will always see *Roar and More* as the seed, the instigation, of my ever-growing library, which threatens the beams of the house where I live now, a house built in 1820 for a cabinet-maker, not for a little girl who always knew that whatever she grew up to be—anthropologist, artist, novelist, mother—books would fill her walls, her basement, her attic: every corner of her colorful life, not to mention her heart.

Das Kapital

SHAHRIAR MANDANIPOUR

I miss my library at my home in Iran. There are books there about which I could write beautiful memories. Where I bought them, where I read them, and what pleasures and sorrows I experienced from them. But I can't go home. I am a writer in involuntary exile.

There used to be a book in my library that caused quite a bit of trouble for me. It was 1979. I was twenty-one and studying political science at Tehran University. It was the days of the Revolution. In cities across the country people had taken to the streets. They were shouting "Death to the Shah" and braving tear gas, batons, and bullets. They were being wounded and killed and the next day an even greater number of them would pour out onto the streets. SAVAK, Iran's terrifying secret police, was paralyzed. I remember it was a beautiful, doleful autumn day. Tehran University's old sycamore trees had lost their leaves and the crows' nests lay exposed among the naked branches. In their long lives these crows had witnessed many scenes at Iran's oldest university—scenes of students demonstrating against the Shah, of them being beaten and killed.

I walked out of the university and found myself facing tens of street peddlers on the sidewalk selling books whose titles we had for years only whispered to trusted friends—books that only a few months earlier, if found in our possession, could have brought us years of imprisonment or a death sentence. It was beautiful and frightening. Censorship had been defeated by the Revolution. Freedom was at hand.

I bought Prophet Marx's *Das Kapital*. It had a plain white cover with only the Farsi translation of the title printed on it. It was a book that for years I had read about in leaflets circulated under the cover of night. I knew it had been published underground and that some had been tortured with hot irons for owning a copy of it. With the feeling of having committed a revolutionary act, I shoved *Das Kapital* in between my university textbooks and headed home. I was eager to read the book that had launched tens of revolutions in the world.

The country was under martial law. Throughout the city, soldiers and officers in American Reo army trucks lay in ambush for revolutionaries. Walking down Farvardin Street I was stopped by one of them. A lieutenant approached me and demanded that I identify myself. My heart was bursting with fear. I thought, I'm done for, I'll be arrested and tortured into confessing that I'm a communist and a member of a guerrilla group. I explained to the lieutenant that I was a student at Tehran University. He took my books and began inspecting them: *Constitutional Law of Iran*, *Labor Law* . . . and *Das Kapital*. He leafed through it.

Iranian radio and television channels regularly broadcasted speeches and oratories against Marx, so much so that many believed Marxism was a plague. That lieutenant, too, must have heard of Marx. Fortunately Marx's name appeared nowhere among the pages. "It's about economics," I told him. "Part of my university course work." He read a few sentences—all about capital, profit, and labor. He returned the books to me and said, "Well done, boy. Go study."

Overjoyed at having escaped arrest, I hurried home. I started reading *Das Kapital*. I kept reading, but I couldn't understand much. Eventually, I gave up on it, or perhaps it gave up on me. Although my father was a successful businessman, it seemed I had inherited none of his financial acumen. Still, in the weeks and months that followed, I was proud to see it there in my library.

The Revolution triumphed. For roughly two years we enjoyed freedom. Then dictatorship set in. To add to the hard luck of the Iranian people, Saddam's army, supported and encouraged by Western governments, invaded Iran and razed and ruined towns in the south and west of the country. Saddam's goal was to occupy Tehran in three days, but the people's resistance crippled his army. The war gave the Islamic regime yet another excuse to intensify repression and execution of its opponents.

I joined the military. I could have been posted to a base where I would be assigned to training soldiers, yet I volunteered to go to the front. Apart from a strong sense of nationalism, I was driven by another motive. I wanted to become a writer, and I wanted to experience war so that I could write about it. But the base commander shipped me off to Kurdistan province. Iran's Kurdish population had revolted against the Islamic regime, and communist groups were strongly active in the region. It was a civil war. I knew I could not kill my fellow countrymen. I escaped from the front, returned to my hometown of Shiraz, grew a moustache, and started living a clandestine life at a relative's house. At the time, the Islamic Republic readily executed young people who were found only to be in possession of a single anti-government leaflet. I was an army lieutenant, a deserter from the front—from the fighting in Kurdistan, to top it off. My circumstances were dire.

Only a few days of my life in hiding had passed when I remembered *Das Kapital* sitting in my library. If the secret police raided my house, the book would be excellent evidence that I was a diehard communist, a supporter of leftist factions in Kurdistan, and an infidel defiant of God. My sentence? Execution, of course.

I scrutinized my face in the mirror. I didn't have a thick Stalinesque moustache. It was quite thin. Still, I convinced myself that I wouldn't be recognized and that I could briefly visit my home, taste the pleasure of Mother's kiss, and touch my beloved books. Their spirit and the soul of their authors were like Eugène Sue's *The Wandering Jew*. I had this book in my room, too. In a way I was like Ahasuerus—with no affiliation to any political group, yet in danger of the most severe political accusations. I started burning all my anti–Islamic Republic books and journals. I congratulate you if you have never seen smoke from a book-burning. It is a heartrending, dark smoke. It is similar to smokes that have risen from plague-infested cities.

I burned many of my books. At last I reached *Das Kapital*. It wouldn't have burned easily. It was very thick. Ah, couldn't Marx have written more concisely? Of course, that's not what kept me from throwing it into the flames. I simply didn't have the heart.

I packed the book in a suitcase together with tens of novels—among which were a few socialist realist works such as *Chapayev*—and took it to a friend's house. He was an ardent revolutionary and a fervent Muslim and had played an important role in the success of the Islamic Revolution. But because he was an honest man and not interested in thievery and exploitation, he had been ousted from his position a few years after the Revolution triumphed. *Das Kapital* was most certainly contrary to his religious beliefs. (Such contradictions occur only in countries such as Iran.) It was a symbol of infidelity and ungodliness in the house of a devout Muslim. However, this particular devout Muslim had a master's degree in electrical engineering from one of the best universities in Iran. We were good friends. He agreed to hide my suitcase.

Months passed. I learned that my squadron had been transferred to the frontlines of the war with Iraq. It was a senseless war—as senseless as the war in Vietnam. Nonetheless, I went to the base and explained that I wanted to return to military service. Once again a lieutenant, I fought on the first line of defense for eighteen months. I survived that bloodiest of wars and returned to the house with a library that held translations of hundreds of the world's most important books and novels, but no *Das Kapital*. I started to write.

Depending on the political climate, Iran's censorship apparatus would occasionally ease restrictions on books and I was able to publish my works. They were well received by the public. I was on my way to becoming a prominent writer and a thorn in the side of the Islamic Republic, an anti-regime writer. And I continued to write without *Das Kapital* in my library. It was demeaning. This was a book that I should have had the right to own.

My friend would occasionally call me and plead, "Shahriar, my own political circumstances aren't all that great. Your suitcase could get me into a lot of trouble. What should we do with it?" And I would say, "We'll think of something." I never did. I still didn't have the heart. Much as I didn't like or understand *Das Kapital*, I couldn't take back and burn that for which thousands had sacrificed their lives. I wanted the book to remain there, in that suitcase, under my friend's bed or in his cellar or buried at the back of a closet, even though it could pave our way to prison and the gallows.

In my library, the spaces once occupied by *Das Kapital* and the books I burned remain empty. The whisper of their souls and that of their writers is no longer amid the murmur of the other books. My advice to you: If you buy a book in the Prague Spring that arrives in the wake of a revolution, do so carefully.

—*Translated from the Farsi by Sara Khalili*

The Viking Portable Dorothy Parker

J. COURTNEY SULLIVAN

The book was a sixteenth birthday present from a witty and eccentric high school friend named Arden. She was only a year older than I, but she had much older siblings, a fact that gave her an air of sophistication. She was that friend every teenage girl needs to steer her in the right direction, to put the world in some sort of practical order. *Woody Allen: He's really really funny. Stirrup pants: You just can't wear those anymore.*

For my fourteenth birthday she had presented me with a book on scandals of the Amish, which I cherished; for my fifteenth, an oversized tub of brussel sprouts wrapped in lingerie, which I hid under my bed. When I turned sixteen—that day when one is supposed to be festooned with pink ribbons and sugary icing flowers—Arden arrived at my door with a thick, unwrapped paperback: *The Viking Portable Dorothy Parker*. The cover intrigued me: a black-and-white photo of a pretty, short-haired woman with dark eyes, looking broodingly, longingly, off into the distance. "Dorothy's our people," Arden said with assurance. I nodded. We weren't really the sweet sixteen type.

I quickly learned everything I could about her: Parker was born in 1893 and had a fairly miserable childhood, losing her mother when she was very young and then getting shipped off to boarding school. She wrote smart, dark, and funny, and was all of those things in real life, too. She attempted suicide several times. She was married three times (twice to the same man). In the 1920s, she and a group of writer friends formed the Algonquin Round Table, that most talked-about of literary circles. In later years, she was put on the Hollywood blacklist and descended into alcoholism. It wasn't a very happy-sounding life, but I was instantly obsessed. I loved the book before I'd read a single sentence.

The word *portable* in the title was fitting. Twelve years have passed since I received it, and the paperback has traveled with me everywhere I've been. Books are like family members, like friends. They go with you, and more than a couch or a quilt, they represent home, the familiar. At least they do for me. Others in my collection are more pristine, more beautiful. There are several dozen hardcovers on my bookshelves now, and even a few antiques. But this book bears the marks of love: a cover that's fraying slightly at the edges, pages with a sun-stained border, underlinings in pink and blue and purple ink, some straight as an arrow, which I'm sure were drawn in bed. Others wobbly and disjointed, hastily written on the subway. There are the margin markings, in my own sort of shorthand: exclamation points, meaning, roughly translated, *HA*. A single check mark, meaning *I wish I'd written that.*

Looking it over, I can tell you at exactly which stage of my life each of these markings was made. I didn't read the book straight through, beginning to end. Instead, I discovered it part by part, according, I think, to what I could handle at any given point. (Not unlike those designer Swedish high chairs that everyone in Brooklyn seems to have now—*your baby can sit in this booster seat before he's even able to hold his head up, and then later he can convert it into a futon to use in his college dorm!*)

First, of course, came the parts about love and angst, not necessarily in that order. In high school, I adored Parker's witty little poems, her tart and cynical musings on romance, which are interspersed with essays and stories throughout the book. (Perhaps speaking to my adolescent attention span, I hardly noticed most of these longer pieces then.) My friends and I developed a Tao of Parker when it came to boys. (Anyone who knows something about Parker's own love life knows what a smashing idea this was, but anyway.) Examples: "Never say to him what you want him to say to you." And the equally instructive but far less useful:

> By the time you swear you're his,
> Shivering and sighing,
> And he swears his passion is
> Infinite, undying—
> Lady, make a note of this:
> One of you is lying.

I memorized and recited the poems as I rode the train home from school or loaded the dishwasher after dinner. I took three years of high school French, and don't remember a word. But I can still do most of *Enough Rope* from memory.

One night while my parents were out, I wrote a few of my favorite Parker poems right on my bedroom wall. I copied "Observation" above the headboard of my canopy bed:

> If I don't drive around the park,
> I'm pretty sure to make my mark.
> If I'm in bed each night by ten,
> I may get back my looks again.
> If I abstain from fun and such,
> I'll probably amount to much;

But I shall stay the way I am,
Because I do not give a damn.

Strong words. Especially, as my mother pointed out, when you write them in Sharpie on your ballet slipper–themed wallpaper.

The thing was, I gave a damn. I was pretty obedient by normal teenage standards. I came from a relatively functional family. I had had the same boyfriend, of whom my parents approved, for three years. I never smoked or drank. I was nothing like Dorothy, really. And this was perhaps one of the reasons I loved her most. For a certain kind of girl, Dorothy Parker is the human expression of wit and spunk and strength and rebellion. The same way generations of new kids are always discovering the music of Kurt Cobain—thinking they're the first, or if not, then at least the ones who truly understand it most—girls like me discovered her. In doing so, I imagined another sort of life for myself. A life in which I gallivanted around Manhattan without fear, making pithy remarks about this or that, always knowing the right thing to say at the right time, instead of thinking up the perfect comeback two days too late.

All through my junior and senior years, *The Viking Portable Dorothy Parker* sat on my dresser or in my backpack, a sort of talisman. By then I had decided that I wanted to be a fiction writer in New York City some day. Preferably 1925, though I was willing to cede that part of the wish.

In college, I kept the *Portable Parker* on my nightstand, and fell in love with her short stories while I was supposed to be reading Milton. She was the sort of exquisite, clever storyteller with whom you could stay up all night. Her characters had names like Mimi and Midge, and their observations were razor sharp. In "The Lovely Leave," a woman's soldier husband comes home just for an afternoon and she is cross with him for leaving so soon. "I like you in black," he says, complimenting her dress to keep the peace. She replies, "At moments like this, I almost wish I were in it for another reason."

Parker and her stories were emblematic of a time I greatly romanticized, and sitting there in my flannel pajamas at Smith College in Massachusetts, I'd be transported to her Round Table at the Algonquin in Manhattan. I could picture her sipping gin and zinging Robert Benchley in a crowd of writers bathed in cigarette smoke. I wanted to be there, too.

After graduation, I moved to New York. I lived with a roommate in a small and charmless apartment across from a fire station, and felt more or less lost in this vast, fast-moving city. Some days I'd look up while riding the subway and it would hit me, not in a pleasant way: *I live here.* I often doubted whether I had the pluck to survive, and since I had few friends, my beloved books became even more important to me, though the only place I could fit them was piled up in the closet. I'd sometimes stand before them, my eyes running over their familiar spines, dozens of familiar novels and biographies and poetry collections nestled in between my bathrobe and suitcase. A select few, maybe ten or twelve, got to live outside the closet, and the *Portable Parker* made the cut. Its contents were a reminder: *You're here to be a writer, this is the city you've been reading and dreaming about for so long.* Dorothy's picture on the front cover was a reminder, too: *Oh please,* she seemed to say. *Quit your whining and just get on with it. You're tough enough.*

This was around the time that I discovered Parker's genius book reviews. Somehow I had never noticed them in the book before. To read her real-time thoughts on the novels of her day was to be a part of the living, breathing world of writers, and I cherished lines like: "*Lolita,* as you undoubtedly know, has had an enormous share of trouble, and caused a true hell of a row." And, "I am sick of those who skate fancily over the work of Mr. Capote, to give their time to the beat boys. They neglect to say one thing, which is, to me, the most important; Truman Capote can write." (There's still a purple Post-it marking that February 1959 *Esquire* review of *Breakfast at Tiffany's*.)

Sometimes I would read the work of the snarky blogger girls who were all the rage when I got to New York, and think that perhaps they were trying for something Parker-esque, but missing the mark. There was that fine line between deliciously clever and just plain mean, and they usually seemed to come down on the latter side of it. I was beginning to get my first newspaper assignments, and I even tried one essay in a tone I thought of as similar to hers. It was an open letter to my book club, declaring that I was dropping out. A lot of readers thought it was funny, but the women in my book club did not. They stopped speaking to me. I never wrote anything like that again.

One spring evening, a few years after I'd arrived in New York, and was just starting to feel comfortable here, I got a chance to have dinner with a young woman writer I admired. I was nervous, and got there early. She arrived ten minutes late, with a book in her hand—*The Viking Portable Dorothy Parker*. "I'm rereading it. A trip down memory lane," she said, with an almost embarrassed smile, like I'd just caught her listening to a Menudo album on her iPod. When I told her of my love for the book, she said that she too—and many others like her—had come to New York wanting to be Dorothy Parker. "We want to write the way she did, without living life the way she did," this woman told me.

Apparently we had all been reading Parker in our suburban bedrooms around the country as young girls, in collective, unknowing awe. But ours was the generation of Type-A perfectionism, even among writers. There's a certain zany, disordered, bohemian lifestyle we all put up on a pedestal, while quietly making our college loan payments on time, and worrying about deadlines, and passing on that third glass of pinot grigio because tomorrow morning's hangover just isn't worth the trouble.

There's no such thing as the modern day Parker, so we worship her in absentia.

Over the years, I've become known to those around me as her biggest fan. And as tends to happen when everyone knows you like something, I've been given lots of Parker-paraphernalia: a few hardcover editions from different decades, a DVD of the film *Mrs. Parker and the Vicious Circle*, in which Jennifer Jason Leigh portrays the title character with a sort of bored affect and an accent that sounds like she has several frozen grapes in her mouth. An ex-boyfriend even gave me a signed copy of the novel *After Such Pleasures*. I adored the gift, but it never seemed quite right. There, in Dorothy's handwriting, were the words *To Marjorie Grogg—With best wishes. Dorothy Parker.*

Marjorie Grogg sounded like the name of a Parker character, and not one the author would look favorably upon. And the signature—so plain and businesslike—didn't seem like the Dorothy I knew. I still keep that autographed edition in a special place, but there's something sort of serious and uninviting about it. I've never actually read the book. I prefer my paperback *Portable* any day of the week.

One of my best friends from college, Laura, helped me move my things into the very first apartment I had all to myself, the apartment where I wrote my first novel. The two of us stood there in a sea of boxes, uncertain where to start. I felt overwhelmed—I was sick with the flu, and the moving men hadn't been able to get the couch through the door. But Laura opened up a box labeled *BOOKS* and started placing them one by one on the mantle. *The Viking Portable Dorothy Parker* was the very first that she unpacked.

The book has come to mean more to me than even the sum of its contents. I prefer the poetry of Yeats or Auden or Millay to Parker's, but if the house were on fire and only one book could be saved . . .

When I agreed to write this essay, I took Dorothy down off the shelf, the blue-etched cover photo as familiar to me as any family picture from the past. I skimmed through and as has happened so many times before, my eyes landed on a section I had never read, never even noticed—the introduction, written by *New Yorker* writer Brendan Gill. He opened with the line "There are writers who die to the world long before they are dead." It doesn't get better from there. Two pages later, he says of the Algonquin Round Table that Parker "*was* one of their leading lights; to be that, she might have said, it would have sufficed to be a glowworm . . . Hemingway, Faulkner, Lardner, Fitzgerald, Dos Passos, Cather, Crane, and O'Neill were not to be found cracking jokes and singing each other's praises or waspishly stinging each other into tantrums on West 44th Street."

I was shocked by his decision to focus on everything Parker wasn't, instead of what she was. What Gill misses in his assessment is the power this woman's words had for me, and others like me, and more teenage girls to come, across decades and cities and worlds.

When I sold that first novel a couple years back, my editor invited me out to have a celebratory drink. We met at the Algonquin.

The Merck Manual of
Diagnosis and Therapy,
Eighth Edition

———

TERRENCE HOLT

This is no time to wrangle but consult
How best we may fulfill the oracle.
Sophocles, *Oedipus Rex*

One day, from the shelf above the leather armchair in my father's study, I pulled out a thin, green-bound volume. Had I been able to read, its title might have been *Infectious Diseases of Childhood*, but to me it had no title. What it had, and what riveted me the moment I opened it, were illustrations. Airbrushed, blandly clinical, on pages smoother than skin and glossier, they depicted confluent pocks and red, bulging membranes, ruptures, eruptions, and suppurations. I stared long enough to register this, and then a moment longer, as incomprehension and disbelief gave way to horror. I was only five: I closed the book, flung it away, and ran.

I still remember the visceral frisson, communicated through the cool sheen of the pages, the smell of ink: it pursued me as I ran. The rest of the day, flashes of those ugly images kept returning. They pointed to some significance I couldn't begin to parse, yet knew was vital, as if life itself depended on it.

From that moment I acquired a certain relationship to books and to meaning that persists to this day.

A few years later, halfway through second grade, I contracted measles. Even through the haze of fever and exhaustion, as the spots spread over my skin I remember staring at them, horrified to find my own body marked as I had seen in that book. The shock communicated from its pages returned, transmuted by fever into rigor and delirium. As I shivered in their grip I wondered, with a sense of betrayal and loss, how the horrifying pictures had actually failed to convey this sense of inner emptiness, this precipice over which I fell and fell.

As soon as I was well enough, I crept into my father's study and pulled down the book again. I needed to know, now that I had seen the marks on my own skin, that the images were not as horrifying as I remembered. Now that I could read, I found much more than that. At the entry headed "Measles" I began to decipher, grappling polysyllables with an intensity I had never felt before. I learned that my illness (what I had experienced as a solipsistic chaos) had followed a well-defined sequence of fever, prostration, photophobia, the eruption of rash, and then intense pruritus, resolving within seven to ten days. Seen through this double perspective of lived experience and rational discourse, the pictures seemed to lose their terror. As illustrations of the text they assumed their proper place: peripheral to what had become a narrative, an orderly account ending not in disintegration but in health.

But this reassurance had its consequences. As I forced my way through the text, I found I had developed a new intolerance of my own ignorance. Encountering a word I did not know—and there were many—I worried at it, doggedly shaking meaning out of it. *Prostration*, even *photophobia* I eventually solved; but when *pruritus* baffled all my efforts I returned to the shelf, looking for another book that could supply what I could not. My hand fell on *The Merck Manual.*

I knew the moment I saw it that I had found something belonging to an entirely different order of knowledge: calm, magisterial, in every way unlike the brute and garish book of childhood disease. I flipped the *Manual*'s pages from front to back and found no painful graphics: only words, densely printed in a crude Century Schoolbook. Grouped into categories identified in gilt letters on black tabs as "GI," "GU," "GYN," "INF," "NER," "NP," each section was a catalog of much more erudite horror, though horror it remained nonetheless. At "Eye," I found "Foreign Bodies," "Lacerations," and "Burns," the last engendering a sick inward squirming as I read. The section headed "Physical and Chemical" treated "Decompression Sickness," "Drowning," and "Venomous Bites." There were sections covering areas of misadventure I had never heard of: "Endocrine," "Neuropsychiatric and Psychosomatic," "Venereal."

On page 1304, I found what I'd been looking for: *Pruritus (Itching). A sensation, generalized or localized, which the patient instinctively attempts to relieve by scratching the skin in the area affected.*

As I read I felt that inner precipice opening again—but now what it revealed was no abyss. It was Revelation.

Not that Itching was itself so great a mystery. I had during my recent attack of measles (Rubeola) suffered enough of it. What *The Merck Manual* offered was a new relation to reading, to narrative, to knowledge itself, redeeming the brute spectacle of those pocked and disfigured bodies. It swept aside the obscurity of pruritus as completely and abruptly as, at the end of time, we are told the sky itself will scroll away. I had glimpsed the machineries of the primum mobile: my material, itchy self, subject to mysterious twinges and fevers, rashes and lacerations, festering, decay, nausea, pain—all, the enormous mass of print promised, comprehended between boards that in their darkness were mystery and death, and in their opening admitted me to knowledge of the same.

For death, I soon came to see, was where the human frame inexorably tended. Not that I registered this at first as applying to me. When looking up measles in the appalling green volume, I had noted how frequently the phrase "vomiting, convulsions, and death" concluded the brief narratives that accompanied the illustrations. And although I understood, indistinctly, that in the worst of cases measles could end in that incantatory sequence, I knew differently: I was still alive. The green book's dire sense of how to end a story struck me as a kind of rhetorical exaggeration, much like what led the mothers of the neighborhood to warn us of BBs and other foreign bodies in the eye, from which, *The Merck Manual* now told me, permanent total blindness may result.

And in teaching me phrases like "permanent total blindness," the *Manual* gave me a rhetoric of dispassionate description in which one could embody any horror one might imagine (and many more one had not). In doing so, it gave those horrors a reality no other voice in my experience, no matter how exaggerated, had touched. This was the double-edged power *The Merck Manual* offered: it promised a kind of mastery over both horror and reality, in words (I already instinctively felt, but would spend the rest of my life coming to know) that only pretended to calm, but in so pretending made themselves more fearful than any amount of shrieking could have been. Words like: Your Daddy's had a heart attack.

At this distance, I'm not even certain this was my mother speaking. It could well have been an aunt, or one of those mothers from the neighborhood, drafted for the present emergency.

The identity of the messenger was nothing to the puzzle the message itself presented. I knew what attacking was: in the adult world it involved shooting, screams, and frequently things on fire. Additional questions—what might attack a heart this way, what happened to the heart—I did not pursue. I may not have wanted answers. In any case, none was offered, just: a heart attack. I was four at the time of this attack—long before *The Merck Manual*; before the book of childhood diseases, too.

I remember much more clearly my father's return from the hospital. As he came up the walk, a two-tone Chrysler Windsor gleaming behind him in the dusk of a May evening, he wore a Stetson fedora, and swung a brown leather briefcase at one side. Behind the round, tortoiseshell spectacles, a goofy smile opening in his face, he looks, when I remember him now, impossibly young. At the time I had no sense of his age, or anything else beyond the simple fact of him, alive and striding through the door.

Only after the fact, with my father home, home but changed, did the event begin to take on features of a mystery—features that deepened with time, as the change his heart attack had worked in him became clearer. The ashtrays and red packs of Pall Malls disappeared. He worked shorter hours, coming home, sometimes, before I was asleep. There was something else, not in him but in us, insensibly present like a high haze dimming an otherwise cloudless day: an anxious hovering. No one discussed it. Years passed, but the haze did not disperse.

Dread sustained like a long-held breath, sustained as well by silence: if anything could dispel that silence, I realized, it was the dispassionate speech of *The Merck Manual*. I had discovered the *Manual*'s extraordinary power to make sense of measles. Perhaps it could master other realities too.

Balked, at first, by the absence of "Heart Attack" from the index, I turned to the start of the section headed "Cardiovascular" and dug in. I labored at it daily. Pick-and-shovel work might have been easier. But at "Angina Pectoris" I knew I was close. Before "Myocardial Infarction" I wavered a moment, looking beyond its inscrutable title to the next section, where "Congestive Heart Failure" beckoned. But immediately below "Myocardial Infarction" I found: *Damage to a portion of the heart muscle by myocardial ischemia usually resulting from occlusion of a coronary artery, and characterized by severe substernal oppression, shock, cardiac dysfunction, and often sudden death.*

Much of this I could not understand, but it told me enough that I pressed on. In "Signs and Symptoms" I read: *The patient appears to be in acute distress.* I imagined my father in acute distress, wringing his hands, clutching his chest as he felt a squeezing, pressing, or constricting sensation. *The crushing pressure on his chest prevents him from breathing properly. . . . Nausea, vomiting, hiccups . . . extreme weakness and fear of impending death. . . .* I struggled through this, feeling constriction in my own chest as I read: had it not been for the calm clarity of the prose, I doubt I could have read on.

"Clinical Course and Complications" promised not only to explain the past but to foretell the future. *It may be insignificant; it may cause sudden and apparently painless death; or it may be prolonged, hazardous and complicated. . . . The majority survive the first 2 or 3 days . . . but then either slowly decline or improve. . . . If the patient survives the first 3 weeks, he is well on his way to a convalescence relatively free from hazard.*

I was at most eight or nine, and did not know to call this *oracular* or *gnomic*, but if those words had been offered I would have embraced them. If anything was clear, it was that the oracle spoke in riddles. Imagining my father vomiting in fear of impending death had been almost intolerable. But the longer I listened, the more the oracle seemed to be speaking about me as well. As I read about my father's heart, I could not help listening to my own. Over my early teen years, as I continued to consult it, the possibilities grew worse and worse: "Acute Gastric Dilatation," "Cryptitis," "Enuresis": surely I had all of these. "Toxemia," "Amebiasis," "Cirrhosis," "Tuberculosis of Bones and Joints": all joined hands in a danse macabre, a differential diagnosis of me that, the longer I wandered through the *Manual*'s pages the more clearly I realized, included everything.

At some point, repression triumphing at last, either I put the book away for good or some other hand removed it permanently from the shelf. It disappeared, and did not return until much later, when, after college, an aunt gave me a more current edition. The heft of the black brick had not changed; the thumb tabs along the fore-edge still bore the same gilt glyphs. The familiar darkness drew me in again, and in that dark wood I wandered, lost, until I strayed into the conviction that a paræsthesia in my left leg must be incipient Lou Gehrig's disease, and there for some weeks I remained, stuck in a Hell of my own making. This was on the way to becoming a doctor. My first encounter with a man dying of it convinced me I did not have Lou Gehrig's disease. After that, when I opened *The Merck Manual* it never referred to me. And after a few years, as medicine became less a mystery and more a settled practice, I never opened it at all.

When I was asked to write about a book, one book that had been important to me, out of the deep *The Merck Manual* surfaced again. It was chastening to find it there, shouldering aside *The Odyssey*, the Bible, even *Moby-Dick*. I was unprepared. This? I thought. This reference work? But the fact of it was undeniable. Long before I read any of those others, I knew it as the most compelling narrative of all.

I have done my research. At the library I sought out the long-outdated edition that had also been my father's. I open it, reminding myself that I read as a doctor now. I will find a demonstration of how far we have advanced. Medicine is different now.

As I turn the pages, the differences are immense. Of the drugs I routinely prescribe, the pharmacopeia of 1950 knows only half a dozen. Of the chronic illnesses I see daily, many were in 1950 of unknown cause, untreatable, and quickly fatal. I turn to the same pages I first saw in the last century, and am astonished at how little help there was for acute myocardial infarction. Where now we snake a catheter into the living heart, in 1950 treatment consisted of bed rest, light diet, and oxygen. My reading becomes a triumphal procession.

It is in the chapter immediately following "Myocardial Infarction" that the triumph begins to falter. When I first saw these pages, looking long ago for explanations, this chapter on "Congestive Heart Failure" had almost drawn me. But once I realized that myocardial infarction was indeed what my father had acutely suffered, I thought I knew all I needed, and never read on. Looking back now on the thirty-six years of my father's decline, I understand that I should have read it all: much of that later history had been shadowed forth within those pages on failure, even to the weeks before his death, when secondary cerebral anoxia leads to insomnia, poor mental function, delirium, and coma. The *Manual* laid out the whole progression, down to its last sad effect, which he himself recognized a year before he died, after he awoke one night acutely confused. When my mother asked him what this episode might mean, he replied: It means I'm not getting enough circulation to my head.

The problem with oracles, as the Greeks keep trying to tell us, is that foreknowledge never helps. With self-knowledge we may understand what our story means; but the ending remains beyond our power to change or even know.

The book knows. As it knows my cholesterol levels, my blood pressure, my body habitus, and everything else I inherited from my father, along with hair and eyes and the quirk of mouth I see mirrored in my children. I hold in my hand the story of my own life, too. In one of its chapters the ending of my story is already written. I just can't read it. Not yet.

But the book knows.

For Whom the Bell Tolls

PHILIPP MEYER

Because my parents hate being called hippies, let's just call them bohemians. My mother was and still is an extremely talented artist, whose career was interrupted for twenty years by the need to keep our electricity on. My father, a jack of all trades, didn't start down a serious career path until his late thirties, when he decided he was going to teach college biology. Both had graduated from NYU, my mother in the 1960s, with a degree in English, my father in the 1970s, shortly before he started graduate school at Johns Hopkins.

Apparently graduate stipends were as small then as now—we drank WIC milk and lived in a crumbling, blue-collar neighborhood that was walking distance to campus. Frank's Bar was five doors down and several nights a week a spectacular fight would spill out into the street; all the neighbors would gather on their porches and watch until the Paddy Wagons came. The arrival of the Paddy Wagon was a cause for great excitement among the neighborhood kids. It meant something serious was going on. We'd point and exclaim, "There's the Paddy Wagon!" or "Uh oh, it's the Paddy Wagon!" We also played games like Doctor and Nurse, but frankly the Paddy Wagon always held more interest to me, which is probably why I was not a father at age fourteen, like many of my childhood friends.

Unlike my childhood friends, I grew up with a lot of books, though I took it for granted at the time; they seemed more like furniture, the way debutantes must think about nannies or diamonds. Books were everywhere in our house, stacked on floors, falling off the shelves, propping up tables and chairs. Many of them held great promise until you actually read them: the one called *Ulysses*, for instance, which I thought was about a Greek warrior, turned out to have nothing about battles, running-through-with-swords, or scantily-clad women. In fact, it was possibly the most boring book I'd ever picked up, and I did not understand why we had three copies (my mother's, my father's, and someone else's). Most of our reading material was disappointing like that. I remember sneaking *Tropic of Cancer* up to my room—the back cover proclaimed it had been "banned for obscenity"—but it too turned out to be a dud. The kids in my neighborhood began shouting "fuckshitpissasscunt" at about age three, which made Miller's mention of the c-word once per page a decidedly ho-hum event.

No, the first book I was in love with was not a real book at all, or not what a teacher would have called a real book. It was *Chilton's Guide to Automotive Repair*, a large blue hardback approximately nine hundred pages long. It was the one toy, the one object my parents could not take away from me. I began reading it in my crib at age eighteen months, or twenty-four months, or however old you are when you live in a crib. I will admit it was possible back then that I was only looking at the pictures. I don't quite remember learning how to read; it seems to me like walking, or making poo in a porcelain bowl instead of in my own pants—something I've always known how to do. So perhaps the Chilton family is responsible for that.

The second book I was in love with, by which I mean the second book I remember having any significance in my life, was

John Steinbeck's *The Pearl*. This would have been second grade, in Mr. Quigley's class at Roland Park Elementary, the public school in the rich neighborhood that the wealthy people tolerated, but didn't send their own kids to. It was bounded to the north by Gilman and to the west by Roland Park Country School. The kids at Gilman and RPCS, as it was called, all had to wear uniforms, which made them, as far as we were concerned, a bunch of fucking pussies and retards. Later, they would own the banks where we were employed as tellers, but at the time that was neither here nor there. As for *The Pearl*, I would sit with my head down reading it under my desk—a theme in my life—while the rest of the class was doing something trivial, like taking a midterm exam. Then I would look up and the room would be empty except for me and Mr. Quigley.

"Go on to recess," he told me. "You passed."

The next time this happened was the seventh grade. That year I should have failed three classes (which means you automatically repeat that grade), which is quite an accomplishment in Baltimore City Public Schools. Luckily, Dostoyevsky saved me from this embarrassment—Dostoyevsky and Mrs. Ritz, my seventh-grade English teacher. My grades in her class were, to be generous, subpar. I remember this quite clearly because Mrs. Ritz kept a large chart at the back of the room with all our grades on it, a sort of precursor to a spreadsheet. At the end of each quarter she'd make each student stand up, walk to the chart, and announce his or her GPA to everyone—an average of homework, tests, etc. Mrs. Ritz would then record the grade in her notebook.

When it was my turn, I went to the chart and announced my average. It was a percentage out of one hundred. "Sixteen," I called out. Which was actually a slight exaggeration. My friend Umar Hamid thought the discrepancy humorous and pointed it out to the class: "His ass didn't get a sixteen! He got a nine!"

A few weeks later, I was sitting in Mrs. Kutzer's biology class (which I failed for the year, along with algebra), when Mrs. Ritz appeared at the door.

"Mrs. Kutzer, may I speak to Philipp?"

Of course she could. I was a well-known delinquent and the class watched with interest.

"I found this in your desk," she said. "Is it yours?" She was holding *Crime and Punishment*, another of my parents' books I was reading under my desk but had accidentally left in Mrs. Ritz's classroom. Lest I be accused of snobbery, I should confess that I barely understood it. But as it was about an axe murderer, I found it much more interesting than Stephen Dedalus, who I found then, and still find now, to be a bit self-involved.

"Yes," I said. "It's mine."

"Were you reading it in class?"

"Wellllll . . . "

"Were-You-Reading-This-Book?"

"Yes," I finally said.

She looked at me for a long time, and her face definitely changed. It was the change from "you are a serious fucking idiot" to "you might be okay with me."

"Fine," she said. "Here you are."

That was how I passed the seventh grade.

Which brings me to my real point. All books, as far as I was concerned back then, were basically interchangeable. Chilton manual = *Crime and Punishment* = Anaïs Nin (who, for the record, is boring as hell compared to *Penthouse*). I was not one of those kids who discussed literature with his teachers, nor did I write long diary entries imagining I was a young Kerouac or Goethe. In this way, being an undisciplined kid in a public school was probably a blessing—my approach to literature was basically free of self-consciousness or snobbery. Luckily I was able to learn those things in graduate school.

But at sixteen, when the suckers at Gilman and RPCS were taking the SAT for the fifth time, I was on top of the world. I'd dropped out of high school, had gotten a GED (the equivalent of a high school diploma, my mother told herself) and a job as a bike mechanic. For the first time, the world made sense. I continued to read, still trolling my parents' bookshelves, hunting for works that maybe I'd dismissed as a child but might appreciate now that I had my driver's license and was all grown up. That was when I came across another book from my parents' NYU days, a worn-out paperback copy of *For Whom the Bell Tolls.*

I'd probably just finished reading *The Stand* or *The Hunt for Red October*—the sort of books that my parents didn't own—and a war novel was right up my alley. But when I finished *For Whom the Bell Tolls*, I knew it was something quite different. I couldn't quite describe why, other than it seemed to me that the people described in the book might be real people, and acted as real people might (even if the rendered Spanish they spoke was a bit stilted). They had complex and often contradictory thoughts and feelings. And though there were plenty of battles, what mattered most were the internal lives of the characters—the external struggles followed from the internal ones.

So while I continued to read popular novels, I became more picky about them almost overnight. Stephen King seemed to hold up, but it was harder to return to Tom Clancy or Michael Crichton; at one point I would have felt terrible saying this in public, but Crichton is gone and Clancy now has others write his books for him. My experience with Hemingway, which had occurred not on the terms of my schoolteachers (which carried the associations of *you are being forced to do this*) but simply by my own discovery, changed me. It was not overnight, but it was noticeable—I became more reluctant to believe in simple characters, more likely to rebel at purple language. And while I still appreciated a good plot, I also wanted internal struggle. Reading Hemingway showed me what the best books do: they describe people as they really are—as people—rather than fairy-tale heroes.

All of these experiences were predicated on the physical existence of objects called books. On the ability of a child to sort through his parents' library and, over the course of decades, absorb whichever lessons he is ready to learn. Even at thirty-five, I still pilfer books from my parents' shelves—a few months ago it was Kandinsky's *Concerning the Spiritual in Art*, a book I now find fascinating but just a few years ago never would have touched.

It is hard to imagine that I would have had anything remotely resembling this relationship to literature if my parents had all their books on a Kindle, laptop, or other electronic device. In the first place, you do not borrow your dad's laptop—there are pictures of your mother that he does not want you to see. In the second place—and I feel compelled to point out here that I'm a reasonably competent person, that I can, for example, remove and reinstall the transmission in a pickup truck—I still can't figure out how to listen to the iTunes music I bought five years ago; I've either lost the password or copied it onto too many computers, phones, or pods. And I certainly can't read the papers and journal entries I wrote in 1998 or 1999—the hard drives are in landfills, the floppies are no longer readable, and the formats are not compatible anyway. And yet my mother's hardback copy of *Ulysses*, the one she read and annotated at NYU in the 1960s, the one that about seven years ago made me realize Joyce was a genius—I recently donated that copy to the library at my graduate writing center. It's forty-five years old, and tattered, but it continues to be read. Whereas my Kindle, forty-five years from now, will be buried in a landfill under approximately eleven million other Kindles.

Books, in the end, are such an advanced technology that we have begun to take them for granted. They are cheap, superhumanly durable, they can be passed on for generations. They outlast cars, pets, and homes. You can, like my parents did, put them in precarious piles in various houses and apartments over the course of four decades, have parties around them, change diapers around them, splash them with paint, have burglars break in and walk right past them. Your high school dropout kids will read them, learn about life, and consider returning to school. Your books, unlike your laptop, e-Reader, or whatever magic device they think of ten years from now, will always be there.

The Collected Stories
of Amy Hempel

KAREN GREEN

They told the wife to watch the sun rise and set, to look for solace in the natural world, though they admitted there was no comfort to be found in the world and they would all be fools to expect it.

I've read a lot of books in this past year, the Year of the Fucking Widowhood. I used to have a window seat to read in, and the morning sun would filter through broad, painterly smears of dog slobber. I had my stack of books there, my bowl of strong coffee, the cashmere wrap from my mother-in-law, and beasts warming their bellies at my feet. The window overlooked a suburban street without sidewalks and, across the way, our neighbor's fortress of oleander that she protected from dog pee with shrieks and shovel-waggling. These days I read in a different location.

This day they were headed for Petaluma—the chicken, egg and arm-wrestling capital of the nation—for lunch.

For a while I couldn't read at all. I considered the Bible. It smelled good, and something about the transparency of the pages was promising, but its requirements turned me off: Faith and good reading glasses. Patience, virtue. Forgiveness.

This is easier, I think, when your life has been tipped over and poured out. Things matter less; there is the joy of being less polite, and of being less—not more—careful. We can say everything.

I'll try not to use the word *survive*. I think I've determined, by trial and error, that certain underlined, highlighted, and dog-eared books, in conjunction with pharmaceuticals, are beneficial after a trauma. What was it the realtor called it? "The Incident." Books can be helpful after an Incident.

In California, the homeowner/seller must disclose, in detail, if someone has died on the property recently. How and where. Apparently, this information was dramatically and inaccurately available on the Internet, but I wasn't looking at the Internet, so I had trouble filling out the form. Yes, I had experienced the Incident firsthand, but had no clue as to how to haiku the particulars into a statement of fact. I asked the realtor, who was a shark with a peaches and cream complexion, if he would write it for me, because of my unsteady hand. For legal reasons he declined, but he was allowed to help me construct the sentence. Here's what he told me to write: "Former husband committed suicide on master bedroom patio via hanging." I counted the syllables on my fingers to see if it really was a haiku. No. I counted how many Friday nights I had lived through, then how many I had left to go, give or take, if I kept smoking.

Sometimes I play dumb when it would be so much better to—*be* dumb.

I was asked to contribute to this anthology because I am the widow, via hanging, of the writer David Foster Wallace, whose writing I enjoyed very much, but whose made-up potty humor songs on a road trip I liked even better. Originally, I thought maybe I could mention him, then respectfully move on to the use of text in fine art, or books as juju, or.

It turns out I'm still not used to this. It turns out the word *widow* is still some kind of a joke. It turns out all roads lead to the same chthonic place, which is itself a road that leads to the same chthonic place.

After he died, people drove up to our house and took photos of our cars in the driveway, then blogged about it. This made the dogs nervous. These were people who liked him, or liked his work. Luckily, I wasn't reading blogs, articles, or even obituaries, I was rereading Amy Hempel.

Later—it's a long story how—Big Guy got a copy of the Coroner's report. The Coroner described Mrs. Fitch's auburn hair as being "worn in a female fashion."

In Los Angeles, the Coroner's Office has a gift shop, roped off like it's a red-carpet event, or the entrance to a legal brothel. The building is old, sporadically ornate, quiet, and in a spooky part of town, but when you enter the shop, an obliging, hygienic employee will ask you if you "need help." The logo for the shop is a chalk outline of a body, and you can purchase baby bibs and car cups and beach towels embellished with this graphic. All proceeds go to Mothers Against Drunk Driving, which is communicated to you the second you sputter and decline the cashier's offer of help. In case you're not in the mood to buy that day, you're handed a glossy brochure—not too glossy—to mull over later. I have it somewhere, I think, but I can't find it. This paragraph would be better if I could find it.

Allegedly, the Coroner's Office, or someone connected to the Coroner's Office, will let the *L.A. Times* know if a person of interest has died in a noteworthy way, so people who liked him or his work can find out about the tragedy before, say, nephews. Nephews and nieces can find out stuff about death via Internet pop-ups. For a nominal fee, autopsies can also be purchased and easily made into pop-ups for online readers.

After F. Lee's death, someone asked me how I was. I said that I finally had enough hangers in the closet. I don't think that is what I meant to say. Or maybe it is.

We had a lot of books, some of them much more loved than others. The best loved were in the worst shape. David wrote in margins, I cut them up with exacto knives and splattered ink on them, the dogs chewed them. After David died, I had a legal obligation to examine each book in order to determine its archival value. Instead, I found myself looking for secret messages in the margins, something that would grant me the equation of reversal, or the equation of acceptance. Mercifully I had a helper, also obligated, who was slightly less unhinged.

I donated everything else before I got around to the books. I tore his name out of them so they wouldn't end up on eBay. His marginalia were adorable and still alive, and we were responsible enough to save them from the Goodwill, but they were inconceivable reading because they breathed and sang and capered.

People did ask me how I was. Well, I got rid of that Euro-trash sport coat. I had room in some chamber of the heart to worry about something else. I put the recycling where I wanted it, I had enough hangers.

"Well, not me, not ever," Wesley said. "I sometimes think this is how depressed the people who commit suicide get. And then I thank God I'm a Leo."

In high school, one of my favorite books was *Revolutionary Suicide* by Huey P. Newton. I still have it. It's a paperback with young Huey's profile on the cover, set against a Chinese-red background. His hand rests against his mouth and chin; he looks calm and beautiful. I have been trying to re-enter his world, but it's slow going—maybe because it turns out he was idealistic, not suicidal (Is that sadder?), maybe because he ended up getting shot in the head in his own Oakland neighborhood, maybe because I was trying to read it on a cruise ship last week, where I had a job. Maybe because at some point irony is not relevant, or profound, or comforting. Here is Huey, not Amy, on death and ambition:

The preacher said that the wise man and the fool have the same end; they go to the grave as a dog. Who sends us to the grave? The unknowable, the force that dictates to all classes, all territories, all ideologies; he is death, the Big Boss. An ambitious man seeks to dethrone the Big Boss, to free himself, to control when and how he will go to the grave.

Huey again, on poetry between friends:

Motorcycle, motorcycle, going so fast; your mother's got a pussy like a bulldog's ass.

DFW, in his sleep: "It's fun to read."

"Doctors can't say 'Oops,'" the doctor said. "Doctors say 'There.'"

The doctor had his costume—the same one Dr. Drew wears, except a little more realistic. I don't know why I was so fixated on his wardrobe, but when I phoned him the morning of the Incident, I imagined he had just put the costume on. Pleats, gabardine, weirdo tie, loafers made to glide soundlessly across filthy linoleum. It was so early. I had made other, harder calls, but the police had strongly advised me to make this one, ASAP. I told him his patient had killed himself. That's not exactly what I said. He said nothing. I heard his kids playing in the background. Other than that, silence. I asked after his kids! I suggested he go play with them!

Months later I paid the doctor his hourly rate to ask him exactly what he was thinking when I talked to him that morning. One of the thoughts he admitted to: "Oops."

I review these things that will figure in the retelling: a kiss through surgical gauze, the pale hand correcting the position of the wig. I noted these gestures as they happened, not in any retrospect—though I don't know why looking back should show us more than looking at.

So the job I had on the cruise ship last week was called "photo stylist," and what I did was dress up models and arrange props for the ship's advertising photography. I brought along my adaptable iron, flowers, something called "glow lotion," and enough elegant lifestyle garb to dress six people in. I also brought my books: Amy, Huey, Alice Mattison, Lorrie Moore, Claudia Rankine. One morning we were doing a casual dining shot up in the Veranda restaurant, and I had dressed the models in beiges and whites and Caribbean blues. They looked how they were supposed to: relaxed, without financial stressors, ready to sip a leisurely latte and tuck into the gourmet breakfast buffet. Propwise, it was a frugal shot, so the photographer wanted a little something more, something that would suggest serious relaxation, like a book.

There's some discussion between art director and client about a Kindle, which is nixed. I'm asked to run down to my cabin and bring back a few book selections. Once the dust jackets are re-moved, *The Collected Stories* is judged to have the best color—a really nice old-school cream. It gets handed to the male model, who is aberrantly pretty, smarter than he looks, and who imme-diately begins to read aloud to the female model, whose interests run the gamut from pirates, to Johnny Depp, to pirate stuff. I am holding a sheet up to help diffuse the sunlight. I can feel my stomach hanging over my pants. The pretend-husband is read-ing from the story "Tumble Home," but I can't hear which parts. Somehow he's found a way to mock it, and his "wife" is laughing her cameo head off, which is great for the shot.

"Are you making this up?" she asks.

"No," he assures her, in a stage whisper. "It's word for word."

A good day. The mound in the road was not cat, but tread.

Mason & Dixon

JIM KNIPFEL

In 1997, I was working as a receptionist at an alternative newspaper in Manhattan. I wrote for them as well, but it was the re-
ceptioning that paid the bills. I was perhaps not the world's
greatest receptionist—I tended to drink at lunch and hang up on
people if I didn't like their voices—but somehow I still held the
position for three years.

One afternoon in late March, a deliveryman showed up at
the front desk and asked me to sign for a package from Henry
Holt and Co. The package wasn't exactly addressed to me, but I
opened it anyway. Way I saw it, I was working the front lines
there at the paper, and part of my job was to protect the editors
from the tsunami of crap that flooded into the office every
week—unsolicited submissions from terrible writers, review
copies of self-help books, and promotional CDs from Latvian
pop bands. If I had to throw myself on these cultural grenades
in order to prevent them from damaging the delicate sensibilities of the editors, well then, I felt I'd done my job. These things
usually went in the trash or over onto the freebie shelf, and nobody got hurt.

Every once in a rare while, something good came in. These I
slipped into my bag and smuggled home. Nobody got hurt then,
either. I was putting myself on the line at that front desk, after all,

and figured I was entitled to a little perk now and again. Besides, those silly editors and their sensibilities would never be the wiser.

Although from the outside this latest package looked like most any other review copy from a publisher, something about it was different. It was thicker than most, and heavier, and that made me curious.

I opened one end of the mailer and slipped out the cover letter. Unlike a lot of press releases, this was just a single sheet, and there wasn't much written on it.

Dear Editor/Reviewer,
The wait is finally over. Enclosed please find your advance reading copy of Thomas Pynchon's latest novel, *Mason & Dixon*.

Something deep inside me began to tingle, then went numb. The numbness began to spread as I continued reading.

You are among a select group of editors and reviewers who are receiving an advance copy of *Mason & Dixon*. Because of the limited number available, this is the only copy that will be sent to your office. Please keep an eye on it.

That was as far as I read.
Oh, I'll keep an eye on it, all right, I thought with an insidious chuckle as I opened my bag and slipped the massive novel inside.

To many people, this letter might've seemed like just another press release, albeit mercifully brief and with the hint of a gimmick. To me, however, it was a Golden Ticket inviting me—one of the lucky few—into Willy Wonka's factory.

The analogy's an apt one. From outside the gates, Mr. Pynchon's novels can seem mysterious, intimidating, even a little frightening. Rumors abound about what really goes on inside.

And then of course there's the enigmatic figure behind it all. Once you cross the threshold, however, you find yourself in a world of wonder and magic and astonishment. There's no telling what might be waiting behind the next door or around the next corner. And it wouldn't be in the least surprising if, at some point, a group of orange midgets started singing.

From the time I was in my mid-teens and picked up a mass-market edition of *Gravity's Rainbow* after hearing so many people describe it as "an impossible book," I was hooked. Pynchon immediately became something more than simply "my favorite writer," or even someone I considered the best of America's post-war (or postmodern) novelists. To me, he was, and remained, The Greatest Novelist America Has Ever Produced, Or Likely Ever Will. Beyond Hawthorne, beyond Melville, beyond Faulkner and Mailer, his books seemed to explode from an almost alien intelligence we mere mortals could only barely begin to comprehend. Even comparing him to other authors seemed a futile game, as he was so much a stylistic category unto himself.

Admittedly, my appreciation of his work was on a much more banal level than most. While the academics wrote long and turgid journal articles analyzing the mathematics of his sentence structure and use of time metaphors, and the obsessive geeks spent their days arguing over the minutest references and stupidly attempting to invade his privacy, I loved his books because the prose was outlandishly beautiful, the stories themselves were captivating, and on top of everything, they were funny as hell.

Yes, I'm a philistine—I read Pynchon novels for the *jokes*.

And now his fifth novel—the first since *Vineland*, seven years earlier—was safely in my bag.

People had known a new novel was coming for a couple years. Long before the title was announced, rumors were already circulating. Most people seemed to think the new book was set during the Civil War, for some reason. The premature speculators always bugged me. Now, even though the title sort of gave it away, I'd *still* know before the rest of them.

Hah!

This was where the first complication stepped forward. My editor gave me the go-ahead to write a review, though I never exactly told him how I got my hands on a copy, and lord knows I never showed him the letter (any question as to how I had suddenly become part of a "select group" of anything, I figured, was best left unasked). But given newspaper deadlines and the desire to coincide the review with the book's release date, I had about three weeks to read and digest all eight hundred pages and turn it into a coherent review.

Under normal circumstances, that might not have been such a big deal, even with a day job and a busy drinking schedule. But there would be another factor to consider, and one I had ignored as long as possible.

When I crawled into bed in my tiny Brooklyn apartment that night, I brought *Mason & Dixon* with me, propped myself up on the pillows, and began reading with the heavy book balanced on my chest.

It took me a few pages to adjust to the eighteenth-century typography and spelling, but once I clicked into it, it quickly became obvious that I was reading something remarkable, a profound and hilarious masterpiece, quite possibly the greatest thing Mr. Pynchon had ever written.

There is a rare and strange giddiness that sweeps over me when I encounter a certain kind of prose for the first time. It happened the first time I read Henry Miller, and Nietzsche, and Celine, and Dostoyevsky, and certainly Mr. Pynchon's other novels. It's a mix of joy, possibility, and awe at seeing what can be done with words. Problem was, I got so excited that my eyes began dancing across the page and on to the next, grabbing at a phrase or a word here and there without pausing long enough to register what I'd read. I was so driven to see what came next that I forgot what came first, so I had to stop and back up. Sometimes more than once.

I was up for a long time that night. When I finally did relent and closed the book, it was with both regret and anticipation. I couldn't wait for the next night.

It was the simplest of pleasures, and one I had clung to since I was very young. Every night when I crawled into bed, I'd grab whatever book lay on the scarred and teetering nightstand and read until I fell asleep. Regardless of how drunk, how sick, how pissed at the world I was, it was something to look forward to, something that allowed me to put the horrors of the day behind me.

When I was in sixth or seventh grade, a rumor began spreading around the schoolyard that I read as much as I did because I was going blind, and was trying to cram as much as I could into my head before the lights went out. Truth be told, I spent a lot of time reading so I wouldn't have to deal with little snot-nosed morons who spread idiotic rumors. But wouldn't you know it, a few decades down the line the screwheads got the last laugh.

In 1989, the doctors told me I was going blind. I can't say I was that surprised. The evidence had been there. My eyesight had never been good, and when I was twelve a blind uncle had told me straight out what I had to look forward to. It wasn't until I was in my mid-twenties, though, that the doctors gave it a name: retinitis pigmentosa, a genetically linked degenerative eye disease. The first symptom is generally the loss of night vision, followed by a slow and irrevocable deterioration of the peripheral vision and a loss of visual acuity. The final result is, of course, total blindness. In most cases, the symptoms don't start making themselves obvious until age sixty or later, but I guess I was one of the lucky ones.

Yet while I had all the classic symptoms early, I could work around them. I could still see some, I could still read, and for a long time I went about my business as if nothing was wrong. Even after the doctors confirmed that yes, indeed, I was definitely chugging along on a freight train to Blindville, I could ignore them. They said I wouldn't be blind until I was thirty-five—still a good ten years away. So why start fretting about it now?

There was no sense that I was in a race against anything—I was just doing what I normally did. Even as the peripheral vision closed in, the acuity slid, and I became painfully sensitive to bright sunlight, I didn't think of it in terms of "going blind." They were all just symptoms of this disease, and I simply needed to adapt to them. (Thinking back on it, how I made it home alive some nights, I'll never know.)

One of the real bastards about retinitis pigmentosa is that it can lull you into complacency. Your vision can remain perfectly stable for several years, then *boom*—over the course of a day or two you can lose a major chunk of what vision you had left. So as time went on, I ran into more things and was having more trouble with small print, but still I wasn't that conscious of it. I was just dealing.

Then along came the mighty *Mason & Dixon*, the novel it seemed I had been waiting my whole life to read.

Initially, the problem had nothing to do with the book itself, or my eyes. What I was really up against was the pressure of that insane deadline. And my cat. Especially the cat—a monstrous, multi-toed, and quite possibly retarded tabby named Guy. It was inevitable. I'd be reading merrily along when suddenly I'd find his enormous yellow eyes staring at me over the spine of the book. A second later, his chin would be hooked over the pages. Before long, here came the first leg. Then the second. Then all twenty pounds of him, slithering over the top of the novel like some hairy, clumsy anaconda, to settle himself between me and the words.

Only after the Guy negotiations had been settled did I notice that it was taking me longer to focus on the page, and that I was losing my place more often.

By page 300, the print seemed to be shrinking on me, so I started bringing a magnifying glass to bed. By page 500, I reluctantly abandoned the idea of reading in bed, moving the operation to the kitchen table. There, under the intense direct light of the table lamp, I could crouch an inch above the page, magnifier in hand, scraping across each line. With sixty pages to go, I had to stop. I had no choice. The review was due, and my eyes were simply no longer capable of working with reflected light on paper. Over a period of three weeks, they'd crashed on me for good.

Mason & Dixon was the last book I was able to read in a normal fashion. To me, it will always be The Last Book, in more ways than one. And even though I wasn't able to finish it, I can't think of a better farewell. I mean, thank god I wasn't reading Harold Robbins. Or Harold Bloom, for that matter.

I wrote a review admitting my failure to finish, but without admitting how frustrated and pissed I was. Eyes aside, I needed to know how the book ended.

Then I had an idea.

I'd owned a few audiobooks in the past, but I never really took them seriously. I listened to them the same way I would a radio play. They never struck me as a valid way to approach literature. Part of that may be because "literature" was so hard to find on audio. Apart from Shakespeare, Jane Austen, and Dickens, most audiobooks—the result of a simple business decision—came straight off the bestseller lists. In short, they were crap. And as if to add insult to, well, *insult*, most were heavily edited in order to fit a three-hundred-page novel onto four conveniently packaged cassettes.

Then, much to my astonishment, after the briefest of shot-in-the-dark online searches, I found it—an unabridged edition of *Mason & Dixon* on audio. Lord knows how that one snuck under the gates (maybe it was disguised as a Stephen King novel), but that old tingle returned. I'd be able to hear the end. Better still, I'd be able to read the whole thing again, in a way. Without even considering the expense (roughly $90, which was no small deal on a receptionist's salary), I placed an order. What had been my last real book would now also be my first *real* audiobook.

Ten days later two large plastic cases arrived in the mail. That night I set up a cassette player on that same scarred, rickety nightstand and inserted the first of twenty tapes read by Jonathan Reese.

Mr. Pynchon's novels present any number of challenges to a would-be audio reader. Not only does he juggle a huge array of characters, but he also sprinkles his prose with foreign names and phrases, scientific concepts, and—most troublesome of all—little songs. An actor could have a field day, but Mr. Reese simply read the words. He didn't give each character a wildly different voice, and he didn't try to sing. It was the best decision he could've made. This wasn't a radio play, after all. Not to me it wasn't. It was a necessity.

I can't say that the book didn't lose something in the translation from print to audio. Part of the experience of reading *Mason & Dixon* was the typography, which of course can't easily be read aloud. While I may never know now if I have lost anything like that from the hundreds of other books I've listened to since, in this instance at least I knew it was there on the page and, as I listened, could hear it beneath the words Mr. Reese was speaking.

It's not the same experience, no. It's not like holding a book and turning pages, hearing the character voices you choose. There's no way to mark favorite passages. But at present, it's the closest I can come to reading. It's all I've got. (I could, of course, have my computer read aloud to me—it's in part how I'm still able to write these days—but I would never subject a book I love to the computer voice treatment.)

Beginning again at page 1, it took me several weeks to listen to the entire novel, but I did, and I finally heard the last sixty pages, and the ending brought tears to my eyes.

On the wall above my desk, although I can no longer read it, is a passage from *Mason & Dixon* that I transcribed immediately after first reading it. Over a decade later, it still resonates:

He thought he knew ev'ry step he had taken, between then and today, yet can still not see, tho' the dotting of ev'ry last *i* in it be known, how he had come to the present Moment, alone in a wilderness surrounded by men who may desire him dead, his Kindred the whole Ocean away, with Dixon his only sure Ally.

And although I can't read it either, that advance copy remains in a place of honor on my shelf, wrapped neatly in plastic. Tucked safely away inside is that Golden Ticket, reminding me that, if only for that one instant, that last book, I was part of a select group.

Emily Dickinson
(Literature and Life)

XU XIAOBIN

Emily Dickinson's first book of poetry wasn't published in America until four years after her death. In China, it took nearly a century longer. To the best of my knowledge, only in 1984 was a Chinese edition of Dickinson's poems made available. It received little notice outside of China's academic circles. In the Foreign Literature volume of China's Encyclopedia, there is less than half a page under the name *Dickinson*.

In 1996, I had a chance to attend a writers' conference in the city of Guangzhou. One night, Mr. Xiao, a publisher, called me and another writer over and mysteriously whispered to us that his house had just produced a small print-run of a Dickinson biography. However, he had only one extra copy. The other writer was quick to grab it. Seeing my disappointment, Mr. Xiao presented his own personal copy to me. After receiving the book—*Emily Dickinson (Literature and Life)* by Bettina L. Knapp, translated by Li Hengchuhn—I skipped most events during the conference and immersed myself in reading about Dickinson's extraordinary life.

She was born in 1830 to a well-to-do family but her relationship with her parents and siblings was strained. Her father paid her no attention, doting instead on her brother, Austin, whom she deeply resented. With her mother, Emily felt it was "impossible to get close." She recalled later in life: "I never had a mother. I suppose a mother is one to whom you hurry when you are troubled." Because of this detachment from her family, she longed to find love. Finally, when she was twenty-five, she fell for a local pastor. Unfortunately, he was happily married. All of this hurt and disappointment, along with a disdain for the hurly-burly of society, led Dickinson to enter self-imposed seclusion at age twenty-eight. From then on, until her death in 1886, she largely confined herself to the bedroom of her home in Amherst, Massachusetts, writing more than a thousand poems and rarely receiving visitors.

I was captivated by what I read, astonished by the similarity of my own childhood and growing pains.

I was born into an intellectual family. My father was a university professor, my mother his college classmate during the 1940s. Back then, for women in China, going to university was a rarity. And so you'd think my being a straight-A student, with teachers singing my praises, would've pleased my mother. Strangely, though, for reasons I've never figured out, I was her most disobedient child—not content with household chores, but in love with reading and full of curiosity about the world.

Books were my best friends throughout my childhood and adolescent years. When I was nine years old and in the third grade, my father bought a new edition of *Dream of the Red Chamber*. Written by Cao Xueqin in the mid-eighteenth century, this masterpiece of Chinese literature—one of the country's four great classical novels, alongside the fourteenth century's *Romance of the Three Kingdoms* and *Outlaws of the Marsh* and the sixteenth century's *Journey to the West*—traces the rise and fall of four families during the Qing Dynasty, the last feudal society in China. The work contains more than four hundred characters; it is so massive that my father's edition consisted of three volumes. "You can read it when you grow up," he told me. Just because he said that, I couldn't contain my curiosity. Each night after he and my mother went to bed, I'd reach to the top of the bookshelf where the set was hidden and read a few pages.

I was thirteen in 1966, when the Cultural Revolution broke out. All schools were shut down. Teachers were beaten. Red Guards rummaged the country and smashed everything standing in their way. Miraculously my family escaped their looting and ransacking. I stayed home hiding from the chaos, spending the next three years—after which time my family was forced to the remote countryside and I was eventually put to work in a factory—reading all my father's books. He had a rich collection. The translations of Russian literature were my favorite: Dostoyevsky's *Crime and Punishment*, Tolstoy's *Resurrection* and *Anna Karenina*, Ivan Turgenev's *On the Eve*—all of which were banned during the Cultural Revolution. Had the Red Guards come to the house, as they did to many unlucky families, not only would my father's books have been confiscated and destroyed but he himself would have been dragged to mass rallies to endure public humiliation.

Mao's crazy political movements also caused widespread famine. Food was rationed. In my family, my younger brother, being the only boy, was protected and favored by my mother, who always gave half of my meal to him. In my mother's mind, her son was much more important than her daughters, as he was to carry on the family line. My mother paid no heed to my frail physical condition. All my good grades meant nothing to her. What made it worse was that I loved my mother, and craved her love in return. This lack of motherly love was a nearly fatal blow to a sensitive child like me. I remember one day when I was eleven or twelve, I ran to a shooting range, hoping a flying bullet would hit and kill me and then my mother would cry over my death. This way, I thought, I would finally receive her love, which did not come to me while I was alive. The image of my mother crying over my dead body often moved me to tears.

Children who are not loved by their parents often create fantasy worlds for themselves. Emily Dickinson did this. So did I. I was a child living in my own imagination, keeping the real world away. Soon after Mao's death and the end of the Cultural Revolution in 1976, I entered a university, where I was supposed to be studying finance but instead lived in the fiction section of the school library. China in the 1980s saw a surge of books by both domestic and foreign writers, and when the country officially joined the Universal Copyright Convention in 1992, still more foreign literature flooded in. I read as much of it as I could—*The Temple of the Golden Pavilion* by Yukio Mishima, *Collection of Short Stories and Novellas* by J. L. Borges, *The Castle of Crossed Destinies* by Italo Calvino, among my favorites—all the while writing novels of my own.

I published my first in 1981, and had written one more novel and four other novellas by the time of the writers' conference in Guangzhou. I was then in the midst of work on a new novel, *Feathered Serpent*, in which a mother arranges to have a lobotomy done on her daughter, who finally becomes obedient to her mother's will. Following her mother's order, she gives her blood to save the life of the only boy in the clan. Before she dies, the daughter opens her eyes and says: "Mother, I've paid back all my debts to you. Are you satisfied now?" It was a book about women in four generations of a family clan set against a backdrop of one hundred years of Chinese modern history, and as luck would have it, when Mr. Xiao gave me his copy of the Dickinson biography, I was going through the most difficult phase of the novel's writing. (A certain historical event in the book was so sensitive and still a taboo in all media in China today that I had to write in a disguised way to be sure the novel would pass the censorship.)

At that time I felt so lonely and crushed by the invisible machine. Emily's inner strength, courage, and wisdom inspired me and helped me understand that solitude was nothing to be feared; it could be enchanting, accompanied by a positive energy. As I returned to Beijing from the conference, my mind was refreshed from what I'd read, and my writing began to flow like an abundant river. I finally realized that the fairness that Emily and I searched and longed for as children does not exist. There is no equality before God! Human life is like a ship sailing to its destination with death, but we have no right not to live a good life just because we know we all eventually will die. Every passenger on the ship has the right to display in full his or her value and thus create a sense of beauty in life.

Many times in the years since, I have returned to that book for reassurance. Now, having picked it up once more and opened the curtain over my bedroom window, I can see the Beijing night after a snowfall. A photograph of Dickinson graces the book's cover. It's said that the photograph, aside from a few shots taken in her childhood, is the only one in existence. She is dressed in simple clothes but exudes a discreet elegance. The pair of eyes on that seemingly ordinary face radiate an inner passion and fierceness, as well as a strong sense of courage and strength.

I think of this American poet who lived more than a hundred years ago. Perhaps she once opened the curtain over her window to look at the moon of Amherst.

—Translated from the Chinese by Joanne Wang

Dungeon Masters Guide

ED PARK

Seated at the end of a long table is a man of average height, neither fat nor thin. He appears to be in early middle age. He wears jeans, a grey thermal underwear shirt, glasses, no socks. Face down on the table before him is a book, the cover obscured. His eyes are closed but he does not appear to be sleeping, rather in a state of meditation or private reverie.

The Dungeon Master should explain that this is none other than the novelist E., who has not published a book in years.

If a character chooses to sit at the table, s/he will see a pair of decimal dice, one blue, one yellow, the digits on each running 1 through 0 (i.e., 10). E. will continue to sit in silence, eyes open but downcast, until the dice are rolled. This can be done once every minute of game time; there is no limit. For each roll, the Dungeon Master should read from the chart below. The blue die indicates the tens, the yellow the units; e.g., if the blue die turns up 3 and the yellow die turns up 6, response 36 should be read from the chart below.

The chart reproduces E.'s rambling conversational style. For any statement, there is a 1 in 12 chance that E. will preface it by propping up the book and saying its title: "*Dungeon Masters Guide.*" If he does say the title, there is a 1 in 4 chance he will say the name of the author, "Gary Gygax," and the publication information, "TSR

Hobbies, Lake Geneva, Wisconsin, 1979." At the end of each statement he will return the book to its face-down position.

After every five rolls (i.e., five minutes), the DM must determine if the character has grown exasperated with E.'s rumina-
tions. Multiply the character's intelligence by 5. This is the
chance (15–90 percent) that the character has received TMI (Too
Much Information) and must make a *saving throw* against insanity. (See p. 83 of the *Dungeon Masters Guide* for the chart "Types
of Insanity.") Note that the *more intelligent* the character is, the
more likely s/he will give up on the conversation.

If the character grows exasperated with E.'s answers, and attempts to attack E., s/he will discover that weapons pass through
him without resistance, leaving him apparently unharmed. After
the third such attack it will become clear that he is some sort of
illusion—a trick of the light, a magic vapor, a hallucination
formed of memory and circumstance.

CHART OF THE NOVELIST E.'S RESPONSES

01–10. *Silence.* Roll again.

11. "This is the book I brought on the plane on my first trip to
Korea. I was not quite eleven years old. I didn't want to bring too
many books, so I brought the one that meant the most to me, the
one I couldn't stop reading. You could start anywhere, ride the
cross-references across its 236 pages."

12. "It's possible my parents bought me the book *for* the trip. I
had never been on a plane before. I had been coveting that book
ever since being exposed to Dungeons & Dragons earlier in the
school year. This would have been fifth grade. The book's still in
pretty good shape, considering how much I read it during the early
and mid-'80s. There's Scotch tape along the spine, where the paper
started to peel. Moderate bumping but otherwise a good, tight copy."

13. "I started a new school in the fifth grade. There were two
kids who introduced me to—or should I say *inducted me into*?—

the game. Johannes and Willie. Both had older brothers, who had presumably inducted them."

14. "Actually the first time I played was at the invitation of a friend named Jason. One Saturday afternoon I went to his house, where half a dozen boys sat around the kitchen table—they were older than us, his brother's friends. The game seemed to take an enormous amount of time to start up, what with rolling our characters into existence, and I remember nothing about the adventure that followed. All I really remember is Jason's dad coming in, looking at us gathered around the table with our dice and graph paper, and saying, 'What is this, gay?' Nobody laughed. I am actually 100 percent sure I did not know what *gay* meant."

15. "In grade school, English class was divided between reading, grammar, and spelling. I liked the first, dreaded the second, looked forward to the last. The vocab book we used was called *Wordly Wise*. There was a whole sequence of them, with an owl on the cover."

16. "At school I loved vocabulary lessons. Discovering new words. I remember distinctly the time we learned the difference between *metaphor* and *simile*—the time we learned what these words even were. The words *themselves* were so interesting. They weren't *shaped* like other words I knew. *Simile* reminded me of *smile* and, in doing so, *made* me smile."

17. "Dungeons & Dragons, particularly the *Dungeon Masters Guide*, was like the phantasmagorical appendix to *Wordly Wise*. My supplementary, self-directed lessons."

18. "The truth of the matter is that though I thought a lot about D&D, and read the books from cover to cover—there were three then four main hardbacks when I was a kid—and subscribed to *Dragon* magazine and longed for various game-related products, I didn't actually play the game that much. I have fond memories of my cousin and I beginning a particular D&D module—as they were called—and having the whole thing disintegrate

agreeably into a sort of free associative storytelling. In other words, the game was at once perfect and barely playable for me. At best it was a prop for narrative."

19. "And really a large part of my attraction to the game was the words that were in those books. The arcane terminology, for weapons and magic, nature and furniture, the qualities that went into making a character—that is, a human being."

20. "Dexterity."

21. "Melee."

22. "Portcullis!"

23. "Kobold. Thaumaturge. Paladin."

24. "Charisma."

25. "Dais. Is it *die*-us or *day*-us?"

26. "Halberd. Wyvern. Homunculus."

27. "Scimitar. Buckler. Chain mail."

28. "Druid."

29. "Machicolation. To wit: 'This is a stone projection which moves the battlement out over the outer face of the wall. It has spaces in the stone flooring which allow missiles to be discharged to the space at the wall foot.'"

30. "Basilisk. Cockatrice."

31. "Lycanthrope. Lick-*can*-throw-pea? Like-and-thrup? I didn't know how to pronounce a lot of these words. Didn't, don't."

32. "Clairvoyance. Clairaudience. I loved those words."

33. "Malevolent. Benign. Benevolent. Malign."

34. "See, Mom? It's educational!"

35. "Some of the words I've never encountered since. Psionics, which was this trippy *other* level of playing in which a character had all sorts of powerful mental abilities. It was distinct from magic—any character could choose to be a magic-user, but psionics was something you either had or didn't, and it was very unlikely you had it. I think there was a 1 in 100 chance you had psionic capability."

36. "I liked how much space was devoted in the rulebooks to a trait that so few characters would have. To a situation that might never come up. Just in case. Worlds within worlds."

37. "The *Dungeon Masters Guide* had charts devoted to psionic combat. Since this all took place mentally, my visual impression was of two parties staring very hard at each other, grimacing, clenching fists in inscrutable anguish."

38. "Psionic Blast. Mind Thrust. Ego Whip. Id Insinuation. Psychic Crush. These were basically the same vague thing. It was Gary Gygax hitting the thesaurus beautifully, coming up with creative ways to dress up a list of figures. Numbers made vivid by sheer range of vocabulary."

39. "I still wonder what a *real* Id Insinuation would be like."

40. "I treasured this level of detail in general. The charts, the randomness, the percentages. You got the feeling that any possible situation that came up in the world of the game would be covered by the rules."

41. "Parasitic Infestation. Wind Direction and Force."

42. "The Colors of Gemstones. Chances of Knowing the Answer to a Question."

43. "Intoxication Recovery Table."

44. "Cubic Volume of Rock Per 8 Hours Labor Per Miner."

45. "Creating a Party on the Spur of the Moment."

46. "It's not even that you would ever need half of these rules—just the fact that they were there, compiled in this book, was fascinating. It was the instructions to creating a world, with plenty of room for improvisation."

47. "It was a book that seemed to hold the secret to writing books, in a way."

48. "Because the game grew out of fantasy books. My favorite section of the *Guide* might be Appendix N, 'Inspirational and Educational Reading,' in which Gygax lists 28 authors who had the biggest influence on the creation of D&D. All but

a few were unknown to me. Most were hard to find even at the library."

49. "I eventually caught up with some of this pantheon: H. P. Lovecraft, Robert E. Howard, Michael Moorcock. But the influence of that list of authors and titles was in the fact that I *hadn't* read them, in some cases couldn't even if I wanted to. A whole tradition was outlined on that page. The titles were enough. Playing D&D could create the adventures like the ones contained in those novels."

50. "The names themselves were magical. L. Sprague de Camp. Sterling Lanier. Manly Wade Wellman. A. Merritt. August Derleth. Fred Saberhagen. Andre Norton. I don't know of a syllabus I've encountered since that has cast such a spell on me."

51. "One of the names was Fletcher Pratt—as I'd later discover, a fellow Buffalo native. I was born and raised in Buffalo, and I was a big hockey fan as a kid. I played ice hockey from the age of six, possibly five. Played street hockey or basement hockey or upstairs-hallway hockey any chance I could."

52. "Inside, we'd use tennis balls. The doorframes were the nets. The wood paneling in the basement buckled from the barrage of wrist shots."

53. "I'd watch Sabres games on TV. I'd watch other teams play on *Hockey Night in Canada*, coming in from Toronto. As much as the games themselves, I liked *HNIC*'s intermissions, when players would shoot at targets strapped to the corners of the goal. Pure skill. I'd imagine their Dexterity scores, D&D style."

54. "My father would take me to Sabres games. Back then the Sabres played at Memorial Auditorium, called the Aud. They just tore it down last year and I remember seeing footage on YouTube."

55. "We sat in the blue seats, the second-highest rung. During intermissions, when the Zamboni made its rounds, I'd study for my vocab tests. My dad would quiz me. Then we'd watch the game again."

56. "Hockey's one of the few sports where you hold something that looks like a weapon. Dressing for my own games, I'd imagine I was putting on armor. Shin pads as greaves. Stick like a halberd, battle ax, pole ax, pike."

57. *Takes off gray thermal undershirt to reveal gray T-shirt.*

58. "There's a funny comic on page 111. A wizard is rolling a pair of dice while a cleric is reading a rulebook entitled *Papers & Paychecks*. 'It's a great new fantasy role-playing game,' says a fighting man to an amused onlooker. 'We pretend we're workers in an industrialized and technological society.'"

59. "I thought this was the funniest thing in the world."

60. "Recently I've been writing a novel. There's this tricky section where it jumps back in time to 1981, and the protagonist, who's like a ten-year-old me, visits Korea with his family for the first time in his life and mistakenly leaves his copy of the *Dungeon Masters Guide* at a historical site. There it's picked up by a secret policeman and scrutinized by security experts in some highly mysterious agency."

61. "A laborious translation takes up a year. The agency is bewildered. Is it a Satanic manual of some sort? A grimoire? A code book intended for infiltrators from the North?"

62. "It can't be just a game. It's too complicated. There must be a cipher, a solution."

63. "'Why was it left on a bench?' the spittle-prone chief keeps asking his hapless team of detectives."

64. "I'm not sure what happens next."

65–69. *Takes out notes for novel in progress. Leafs through, shaking head.*

70. "Look at this cover! It's totally insane. I'm amazed my parents allowed me to read this stuff at all. That they *bought* me this! Check it out. You've got this near-nude fire giant or demon or chaotic evil demigod, muscles bulging, looking rigid as a statue, with weird yellow flames dancing around his body and two

horrible looking horns coming out of his forehead and a set of fangs and a nose like a fleur-de-lis and little inexpressive sunbursts where his eyes should be."

71. "Mom, it's not Satanic!"

72. "The demon wears a necklace and a gold chain and a ring and a bracelet and not much else."

73. "A fighter and a magic-user are in the foreground, the former attempting to slice the demon's kneecap, the latter generating a fireball in his upraised hand."

74. "As if a demon in the buff wasn't bad enough—*What is this, gay?*—he's got a huge sword in one hand and a buxom blonde in a gold bikini flailing around in the other."

75. "It's like saying, a little too loudly: *This is not gay!*"

76. "She's basically wearing no clothes. A bit of blue fabric is sort of covering about 10 percent of her right butt cheek. It's possible she's a magic-user herself—she's got one arm lifted, as if casting a spell."

77. "The darkness of the front cover morphs at the spine to a back-cover vista in which a trireme sails on a sea of blood, an iguanoid creature embraces a baluster, and a vast cloud supports a hectic city of golden ziggurats and minarets, egg-shaped structures, obelisks, a pyramid. A gate in the shape of a shrieking face."

78. "There's a note right after the foreword: 'The book cover painting shows an encounter between three adventurers and an efreet [?] on the Elemental Plane of Fire. The fabled City of Brass can be seen floating over a flame-swept sea of oil.'"

79. "It always looked a step away from nightmare to me. But it had this epic, cryptic quality that made it the perfect container for the ocean of material within."

80. "The *Guide*'s parting text, after the glossary but before the index, written in all caps, begins, 'It is the spirit of the game, not the letter of the rules, which is important. Never hold to the letter written, nor allow some barracks room lawyer to force quota-

tions from the rule book upon you, if it goes against the obvious intent of the game. . . .'"

81. "'. . . as you hew the line with respect to conformity to major systems and uniformity of play in general, also be certain the game is mattered by you and not by your players . . .'"

82. "'. . . you are the creator and final arbiter of ordering things as they should be. . . .' That could be the novelist's credo, no? Or the novelist's futile hope. Arbiter. Order. *Things as they should be.*"

83. "Johannes I hear is doing well. What about Willie? I remember going to his house downtown as a kid, this huge maze of a house, dogs and cats everywhere, siblings and step-siblings, computer games on the Apple IIe, cable movies. We watched *Conan the Barbarian*, *Looker*, some tedious Cheech and Chong thing."

84. "He had a lot of D&D material, plus other games by the same company, TSR Hobbies."

85. "Tactical Studies Rules."

86. "Games or parts of games. Cardboard counters, figurines. Decks with cards missing."

87. "His room was a ruin, like a closet in some forgotten corner of that vast house. I remember staying over one night, getting lost, climbing up a set of stairs that ended in a wall."

88. "There are charts in D&D for 'Wandering Monsters.' I always liked that description. A world of constant action. Stay in one place long enough and you'll meet an ogre with a club, a bugbear with a grudge, a gelatinous cube with nothing but momentum and digestive juices on its side."

89. "When did Willie and I drift apart? Certainly by high school, when he seemed in a perpetual daze. Lost to chemicals, some labyrinth of the self. He didn't acknowledge me, maybe didn't recognize me. The one time he did—the one time I remember—his tone held otherworldly mockery."

90. "When I think of who he was when we were friends, and the last glimpses I had of him as a teenager, it breaks my heart."

91. "But then practically everything does these days. Absolutely anything, if I think about it for a minute, breaks my heart."

92. "I wonder what he's doing now. I could look him up online. His full name was *Wilkinson*, like the razor. I've never met anyone else with that name."

93. "Last night I was trying to visualize the Internet. You're supposed to think it's a *net* or a *web*, a sprawl of connections. I've seen an image of a 'map' of the Internet—like some form of pullulating vegetation. But this seems wrong to me, or it did last night."

94. "The structure seemed more vertical. Think of how you typically begin a session online. Entering through a familiar gate—whatever your browser's home page is. Read some breaking news. Then what? Your favorite sites, regular blogs, Facebook. You do the rounds. You get deeper and deeper, but most often it's a journey of diminishing returns, as it gets later and your concentration flags. You pinball from site to site, certain familiar ones popping up again and again as you wander, like you're walking in circles and seeing the same signpost hours apart. I can't help thinking that it's like exploring a dungeon in D&D, going from room to room, checking for traps and secret doors. You keep on going, one level to the next, in the hopes of encountering—what? Something new. Something charged, powerful, life-changing even. You don't even know what you're looking for when you begin, but you're on a quest. And all the while you're at risk of seeing something frightening, a horror conjured out of the dark by forces unknown. Something you can't unsee."

95. "What if someone wrote a *Dungeon Masters Guide* to the Internet?"

96. "Is the *Guide* a guide to the game or the life? Is D&D a simulation or an entertainment, a game or a world? The book *seems* comprehensive, but of course it can't be. To cover *every* sit-

uation would be impossible. The *Guide* gives, for example, 'the formula for the ink required to scribe a *protection from petrification* spell': 1 oz. giant squid sepia; 1 basilisk eye; 3 cockatrice feathers; 1 scruple [!] of venom from a medusa's snakes; 1 large peridot [?], powdered; 1 medium topaz, powdered; 2 drams holy water; 6 pumpkin seeds."

97. "A fairly involved recipe follows. 'Harvest the pumpkin in the dark of the moon and dry the seeds over a slow fire of sandalwood and horse dung. . . . ' That phrase, 'sandalwood and horse dung,' has never left my head. The point is, this is actually a recipe for *writing recipes*. There is a limitless variety of spells—characters can devise new ones, in addition to the dozens provided—and thus an infinite number of scrolls, an infinite number of recipes."

98. "Gygax cheerfully and confusingly notes that D&D belongs not to the *realism-simulation* school of games but to the *game* school of games. 'It does not stress any realism,' he writes, adding, 'in the author's opinion an absurd effort at best considering the topic!' It stands at the weird intersection of fantasy, simulation, pastime, narrative, and metaphor, which is probably why I can't stop thinking about it."

99. "I keep meaning to read Georges Perec's *Life: A User's Manual.* But I don't, maybe because I want it to be the *Dungeon Masters Guide.*"

100. *Shoots mischievous glance, reveals pair of dice in his left palm, rolls them. Consults Appendix IIB to see what character's response is.*

Sula

SUSAN STRAIGHT

Looking around at my hundred-year-old house, a former farm-house on a dead-end street of tiny bungalows and stucco cottages in inland Southern California, and having attended seven funerals in the past two years, I've already thought about my most prized possessions: What would I want my children to have?

I have so little. No gilt-framed pictures, no expensive furniture (almost all estate sale buys from the neighborhood, antique but cheap in an old funky way), and not much jewelry anyone would care about.

There's the hand-woven piece of material shaped like a folder, with thread ties, enclosing green felt pages that hold needles. My great-grandmother made it, in Switzerland, in the late part of the nineteenth century. My girls have seen me use it countless times, to mend their clothes.

A hand-painted box sitting beside me now, brought also from Switzerland by my mother. She used it to hold hairpins; I keep it full of paperclips to hold together my essays and stories.

The huge Chinese silk floss tree outside my window, covered with horribly sharp thorns, which my brother planted from a seed, saying it would protect me. He has been dead eight years now. I have his Mexican fighting chicken, named Coco, who still lays eggs. Also his sheepskin-lined Levi's jacket, with a spatter of ragged holes from where someone threw battery acid at him, which I wear when it's very cold or I miss him.

A cast-iron frying pan given to me by my mother-in-law, who had been told that a blonde girl might not be able to cook properly for her son, but who believed in me enough to give me the pan, show me how to season it, and then teach me how to fry chicken. My middle daughter, who hates to cook, makes only one specialty: pineapple upside down cake, always using this particular pan, because of her grandmother, who died when she was four.

And my books.

Because I still live in the same city where I was born, and because my mother is completely without sentiment and, being Swiss, likes rooms to be clean to the point of bare, and also because no one else in our family ever loved books, the walls of my house are lined with them, including all the volumes of my childhood.

My three girls have read most of them: the ragged, much-handled copy of *Little Women*, illustrated with bonneted sisters; the ancient copy of *Heidi*, which meant so much to me as I imagined my mother living that life, in the Swiss Alps (she spoke very little about her childhood except to say that when she was ten, her mother's body lay on the dining room table until the funeral in the tiny mountain town where they lived above a sauerkraut maker); the Marguerite Henry horse books, of which only one girl read one book—*Misty of Chincoteague*; the Nancy Drew series that the eldest alone loved; and even two of the first books I ever read, *Raggedy Andy and the Lucky Penny* and a water-stained *Winnie the Pooh*. (They refused to touch *Alfred Hitchcock's Daring Detectives*, circa 1969, which used to scare the crap out of me and which I still love for the gory illustrations.)

The most prized book has to be Toni Morrison's *Sula*. I've lent and given away hundreds of books to hundreds of students and friends and neighbors, to the countless teenagers who come through this house, but I've never lent *Sula* to anyone except my oldest daughter.

I waited years to hand it to her, a great reader like me, waiting for the right moment to put it on her dresser or in her palm and have her say reverently, "This is the book you read every year, the one we always tease you about." But she wanted no part of a book she'd seen that many times in my hands. Not until she was twenty, a junior in college, did I succeed in having her actually pick it up and take it with her. And of course, she said with utter incredulity after she'd finished it, and handed it back unceremoniously, "Yeah, the mother lights her son on fire. And the women all end up alone. Thanks, Mom."

Was I fourteen? I had just met my future husband, in junior high. It was summer. I went to the Riverside Public Library as often as I could because it was quiet, safe, and there were no endless chores. I remember it so vividly—the paperback on the revolving wire rack, with a pencil-marked *A* on the inside first page. *A* for Adult? It was for sale. 75 cents.

I picked it up because the young woman on the cover looked so much like my high school friends, the ones in my PE class where we composed a dance routine to Earth, Wind and Fire's "Shining Star." She has brown skin, a cloud of black hair, a dark-blue floral print dress that looks '70s Qiana-fabric slinky, and a birthmark over one eye. Above her the words say—

SHE IS DIFFERENT,
SHE IS MAGICAL, SHE IS
SULA

Until then, every adult novel I read had come checked out from this library or the bookmobile that came to the grocery store parking lot in my neighborhood every other week. I had checked out

at least ten books a week for most of my life. I had read many novels I didn't fully understand. Chester Himes, John A. Williams. I
found James Baldwin and reread *Go Tell It On the Mountain* again
and again. I drank in Toni Cade Bambara's stories.

But I'd never read anything like this. I thought it was a book
for a girl. I didn't know Sula would drown a child, watch her
mother burn without running to help, steal her best friend's husband, defy her town, and die alone at thirty.

This slim novel—149 pages, the paperback published in
1975—became a dark and luminous icon for me. It was like a
premonition. It made me into a writer, it colored how I became a
mother, and images and words from it unfurl themselves in my
mind—like dye dropped into water—nearly every day, as I stand
at the sink, as I drive a car, as I look at my children. Its cheap
pages darkened to marigold, *Sula* remains on a shelf near my
desk, except for the days that I read it again, annually. I have read
the book at least once a year for the last thirty-five years. I married at twenty-two, and every year until we divorced, my husband would see the paperback, the girl's implacable gaze on him,
her hand under her chin, and he would say, "You reading that
book again?" I would say, "You watching *Shaft* again?" We had
memorized large portions of the dialogue of each.

The first time I kissed him was on the asphalt basketball court
down the street from my house. At fourteen, I had understood
little of the scene where Sula is making love with Ajax, but I
never forgot what she saw:

> . . . the golden eyes and the velvet helmet of hair. . . . If I take
> a chamois and rub real hard on the bone, right on the ledge
> of your cheek bone, some of the black will disappear. It will
> flake away into the chamois and underneath there will be
> gold leaf.

Even then, on the school playground, I studied his face, trying to define it in word-images. His skin was the color of palm bark, brown with red underneath; his black eyebrows were narrow crow feathers; on his cheek a complicated scar like Chinese script from where someone had hit him with a nail-studded board.

Months earlier, I'd been walking down a street with my best friend. She blithely agreed to hitch a ride in an ancient Buick like a dirty white boat. I followed her into the backseat, and a few blocks later, the young men inside turned menacing.

At fourteen, I had understood *exactly* what happened when Sula and her best friend Nel are confronted by four Irish boys on the way home from school, boys who have been hunting them as sport, and Sula pulls out her grandmother's paring knife—

Sula squatted down in the dirt road and put everything down on the ground; her lunchpail, her reader, her mittens, her slate. Holding the knife in her right hand, she pulled the slate toward her and pressed her left forefinger down hard on its edge. Her aim was determined but inaccurate. She slashed off only the tip of her own finger. The four boys stared open-mouthed at the wound and the scrap of flesh, like a button mushroom, curling in the cherry blood that ran into the corners of the slate.

Sula raised her eyes to them. Her voice was quiet. "If I can do that to myself, what you suppose I'll do to you?"

The first time I'd read it, the metaphor and simile went into my brain like the vapor of the PCP-soaked Kool cigarettes my compatriots were smoking that summer. I studied my fingertips. Button mushroom. Cherry blood.

In the Buick, I told the men an elaborate story about my stepfather who was a sheriff's deputy. I described his shotgun, fearlessly looking into their weed-reddened eyes, and said, "Do whatever you're going to do, but when you drop us off, he'll find you and kill you."

My stepfather owned three Laundromats. We cleaned them on the weekend. He had no gun.

They left us on another corner, and my friend said, "You just lied and lied."

Thirty years later. My friend Nicole and I sit at my kitchen table, and while she heats a straightening comb on the burner to tame my middle daughter's hair before a dance, I am reminded of when Sula returns to town after being gone for ten years, visiting Nel's kitchen—

Nel lowered her head onto crossed arms while tears of laughter dripped into the warm diapers. . . . Her rapid soprano and Sula's dark sleepy chuckle made a duet that frightened the cat and made the children run in from the back yard, puzzled at first by the wild free sounds, then delighted to see their mother stumbling merrily toward the bathroom, holding on to her stomach, fairly singing through the laughter: "Aw. Aw. Lord. Sula. Stop."

I am the one burying my face while Nicole says, "I looked at this brotha's picture, the one, you understand, he thought best to put up on the dating site, and I see these rings around his face, and I look again, and he got his damn driver license photo on there. That's the best he can do and he think I'm about to give him a call. 'Cause he's a catch. With his lazy broke ass."

My girls hover in the doorway and narrow their eyes, a little afraid to come in.

Just last summer, my ex-husband and I are in his old white truck following our three girls, packed with two other girls and one boyfriend in my old green minivan on a trip to the beach for the eighteenth-birthday party of my middle daughter, when a highway patrolman begins to shadow the van.

The boyfriend is 6'5", dark skinned, with braids that touch his shoulders and an NYC baseball cap on his head. My ex-husband says, "No. Uh-uh. He's gonna find something. He's gonna pull her over."

The oldest daughter is driving. She has never been pulled over. On the crowded July freeway, the patrolman shouts through his sound system for her to move to the shoulder, and we know she's panicked, trying to cut across three lanes. He herds her there, and we follow. The officer leaps from his car, behind the van, and throws up his hands in a what-the-hell? gesture to our truck, which raises a cloud of dust as we pass them and pull in front.

"I'm not having it. I'm not having it," my ex-husband is saying. He thinks the officer will shoot one of them when he sees the boyfriend. I look in the rearview while the officer slowly approaches the car full of black teenagers on a freeway to the beach, scuffle for my wallet and say, "Don't you get out—I'm going. I'm going!"

It is my job. My ex-husband is 6'4", three hundred pounds. I am the short blonde mom, in the khaki capris and white shirt.

But I think, as I walk into the dust cloud now settling, *Custard.*

I smile wide at the patrolman while he is speaking fiercely to my daughter. I say, "Dang it, is that rear brake light out again?

"Who are you? Why did you stop?"

It is my job to make him know. "I'm her mother," I say. "Her dad and I are following them for a birthday party at the beach. The registration is right there, in the glove compartment. Get it out, sweetie."

And I smile, very wide.

Custard.

My daughters, in the front seats, look angry at him, appalled at me. The boyfriend, in the second bench seat, is stone-faced, impassive, meeting my eyes.

Getting on a train to go South for the first time in her life, Nel watches her mother try to rectify the error of having entered the white-only car—

"We made a mistake, sir. You see, there wasn't no sign. . . . "

"We don't 'low no mistakes on this train. Now git your butt on in there."

. . . Helene smiled. Smiled dazzlingly and coquettishly at the salmon-colored face of the conductor.

. . . There in the fall of heavy brown wool [Nel] held her eyes. She could not risk letting them travel upward for fear of seeing that the hooks and eyes in the placket of [her mother's] dress had come undone and exposed the custard-colored skin underneath . . . if this tall proud woman, this woman who was very particular about her friends, who could quell a roustabout with a look, if she were really custard, then there was a chance that Nel was too.

I heard the word as the dust fell around me, and the eyes of my children and their friends shifted, and as I smiled again and leaned my elbows on the hot metal frame so the officer was partially blocked from the open window.

The business of loving and buying and writing and reading books is not a zero-sum game. Thousands of people might read only on their iPads or Kindles in the future; they may never buy another printed-on-paper novel. Thousands more will never have books; they will tell their stories by firelight and kerosene lamp in a circle of people as they always have (or in our family's case, standing around the oil-drum cooker in my father-in-law's driveway, the barbecue smoke drifting over all the cousins as they talk about a shooting that happened in 1921 or a shooting that happened last weekend, as they talk about how much a nephew loves the wrong woman and she's certain to ruin his life). And thousands more of us will read only books we can hold in our hands and pass on to someone we love or want to educate or even someone we hate and wish would learn something, understand something, *feel* something.

Morrison's words from the first instant made me *see* differently. Made the world controllable with metaphor and simile, made everything a possibility of description inside my own head even while things around me were unutterably dangerous or sad.

Nel and Sula. *"We were two throats and one eye and we had no price."*

The book was on the couch again, while I wrote this. My youngest daughter, fourteen, said, "What's *Sula* about anyway?"

She has seen it on every table, bed, and couch in the house, her entire life. The solemn, hooded eyes of the young woman study her. Does she recognize the guarded, evaluating stare as the one she's seen countless times in the gaze of her aunts, my friends, and me? At a school function surrounded by white parents, at sports events where people study us, at the store where the security guard frowns slightly?

She picked it up and looked at the back cover.

Ulysses

SEAN MANNING

I moved to New York in May 2001, less than a week after graduating college. That hadn't been the plan. Grad school didn't start
till September. I'd been looking forward to one last suburban
Ohio summer with my high school friends. Grilling the $30 filets
mignons we'd get for the price of ground chuck from our buddy
who worked the meat counter at the gourmet grocery store.
Sprawling out on the country club's eighteenth fairway to watch
the Fourth of July fireworks. A whole lot of basement beer pong
and two A.M. trips to the Rally's drive-thru. The Saturday following commencement, though, a family friend who lived in the city
called with a line on a cheap apartment. I had to be there to sign
the lease. I was on a flight the next morning.

The apartment fell through, but I didn't think of returning to
Akron. Something had happened when I stepped off the plane at
LaGuardia, exactly as it no doubt would've three months later.
Everything had changed. Adulthood had officially begun. There
was no going back.

I slept on that family friend's couch for nearly a month. This
was before Craigslist. The only way to find an apartment in the
city was the weekly *Village Voice*. The paper hit newsstands on
Wednesday, but Tuesday the apartment listings were updated on
the *Voice* Web site. I'd sit in front of the computer all afternoon

clicking the refresh button. When the new listings finally appeared, I'd race through them scribbling down names and phone numbers. I still wasn't fast enough. Most of the time I'd get an answering machine that was already full. The few landlords and tenants looking for a roommate with whom I did manage to speak turned me down instantly. They wouldn't even meet me. I had just enough money to pay a security deposit and first month's rent and, busy as apartment hunting kept me, was so far without a job. I divulged this freely. I may have been an adult but I wasn't yet a New Yorker.

It occurred to me to check with my grad school. Sure enough, there was an office devoted to helping students find housing. A couple days later I moved into a loft in Nolita, the downtown neighborhood north of Houston Street, bordered by Bowery on the east and Broadway on the west. The loft was owned by a fifty-something divorcée, a devout Sufi who worked at home as an astrologer. She'd bought it for practically nothing upon moving to the city in the early '70s to pursue painting. Back then the Bowery was still the Bowery. She and her two daughters always had to step over some drunk passed out in the building's entryway. When her daughters moved out, she began letting their two rooms. She didn't advertise in the *Voice*, only with my grad school and a couple others in the city. In the other bedroom was an Israeli actress in her mid-twenties. I'd be sitting on the couch or at the kitchen table and out of the bathroom, fresh from the shower, would walk this girl wrapped in just a towel with her long brown hair all wet. Also sharing the space were two cats—a lazy old Persian and a frisky young tabby. The building's roof had a garden worthy of a spread in *Martha Stewart Living* and a view that spanned from the World Trade Center to the Empire State Building. The elevator was one of those old ones with the hand lever and sliding metal gate. Sheryl Crow lived on the second floor. Every now and then I'd come home or be on my way out and hear her strumming her acoustic guitar and singing.

There was still the matter of income. The previous summer I'd worked in a shoe store, the summer before that in a J. Crew. I could've again sold clothes, or perhaps waited tables. But my living quarters inspired me to find equally exotic employment. I'd come to New York to be a writer. I loved books more than anything in the world. (When I visited Paris during junior year study abroad, the first sight I saw wasn't the Louvre or Notre Dame or even Jim Morrison's grave but Shakespeare and Co.) So I applied for a job at the Strand.

If you've ever visited Manhattan, you've likely patronized that fifty-five-thousand-square-foot, multi-floor warehouse on the corner of Broadway and Twelfth Street with the giant red awning advertising eighteen miles of new and used books. If not, you've surely seen it on TV or in movies—*Sex and the City*, that scene in *Unfaithful* where Diane Lane's character finds her lover making out with some other girl in the stacks. Opened in 1927, the Strand was one of more than forty bookstores that lined Fourth Avenue between Eighth and Fourteenth Streets. By the late '50s nearly all those "Book Row" vendors had folded, and the Strand—still owned and run by the Bass family, as it remains today—moved to its current location. Since then it's been perhaps the city's most steady benefactor of aspiring artists and creative types. Patti Smith worked there in the '70s, along with fellow punk rock pioneers Tom Verlaine of Television and Lux Interior of the Cramps. The staff's shared mien isn't mere happenstance but rather insisted upon by management. In order to be hired, you're given a written test in which a list of titles must be matched to their authors. I got stumped on *The Red and the Black* and *Lost Illusions*—something like that—but still passed, and began working in the basement the very next day.

The basement was where the advance copies were kept. These are books sent to reviewers ahead of publication. When finished, reviewers sell them to the Strand. My job was to alphabetize and shelve them. That's it. I'd grab a stack of twenty or thirty advance copies, sort them into piles by author's last name, file each pile in its appropriate rack, grab another stack, sort them into more piles. . . .

It was so depressing—the tedium but also the condition of the books. Most, it was obvious, hadn't been opened, the publicity notices still sharply creased and tucked inside the front covers. All the hours those authors had toiled, all their months and years of sacrifice, just for some reviewer to hawk it back to the Strand for two or three lousy bucks. Then again, at least they got their books published.

That was another thing that bummed me out. I thought that by just getting into a grad school I was set, my career as a writer all but assured. Apparently not. My co-worker William was a recent alumnus of an MFA program far more selective and prestigious than mine. He'd submitted the novel that'd been his thesis project to dozens of agents. He hadn't heard back from a single one.

By far the worst part of working at the Strand was the heat. Even with their stifling, moving-underwater humidity, Ohio summers had nothing on New York's. The tall buildings and miles of road and sidewalk, all that glass and steel and concrete and asphalt—it trapped and held the sun. Similarly, the Strand's twenty-foot-tall metal racks packed tight with books only served as insulation. It was at least ten degrees hotter in the store. There was no air-conditioning. Rumor had it the summer before some obese customer had died of heatstroke in the philosophy section.

The basement was even more intolerable. There were no windows. A few fans hung from the ceiling but just blew around dust. It was hard to breathe, the air was so thick. I'd sweat just standing still. By the end of my 1:30 to 10:30 shift my shirt and underwear and socks would be soaked. Like William and everyone else in the basement, I counted the minutes till my turn on bag check.

In addition to shelving advance copies, us basement guys had to man the counter and cubbyholes by the entrance where customers were required to leave their bags while they browsed. We would rotate every hour. After we'd been downstairs for so long, the faint breeze each time the door opened seemed an arctic gust, the view of the sidewalk a breathtaking panorama. The other guys would usually pass the time reading, but I'd stand there staring out the door at all the people walking by. A few nights after 9/11 a candlelight procession traveled down the middle of Broadway. When my hour was up, people were still streaming past. But even bag check got old after a few months, especially when I started getting warts on my hands from handling so many grimy plastic shopping bag handles and sweaty backpack straps.

The sole redeeming part of the job—other than the five-minute walk to my and Sheryl's place—was the discount. Employees got half-off everything. And everything in the Strand was already reduced in price. A paperback with a $12 cover price the Strand might sell for $6. I'd get it for $3. In the eight or so months I worked there, I bought close to two hundred books. First editions of Sherwood Anderson's *Dark Laughter* and Joan Didion's *Play It As It Lays*. Early hardcover printings of *Native Son*, *From Here to Eternity*, *Last Exit to Brooklyn*, *Lolita*, *Ballad of the Sad Café*, and *Go Down, Moses*. Commemorative anniversary versions of *Invisible Man*, *Look Homeward, Angel*, and *On the Road*.

I would've bought even more but the limit was six books at a time. And you could buy only once a week, on Friday. If you found something Saturday, you had to wait the whole week, and stow it along with the rest of your haul on a special shelf in the basement.

Early one week I came across a copy of *Ulysses*. I'd tried to read the book in college—not for any class, just on my own—but gave up after about a hundred pages. I had no intention of trying again. The edition was just so good-looking, I couldn't resist: copyrighted 1946; devoid of dust jacket; the emerald-green cover emblazoned with two imposing, black, Art Deco lowercase *j*'s; the text prefaced by Judge Woolsey's district court decision lifting the obscenity ban as well as by a letter from Joyce to his American editor Bennett Cerf detailing the European publication history ("My friend Mr. Ezra Pound and good luck brought me into contact with a very clever and energetic person Miss Sylvia Beach who had been running for some years previously a small English bookshop and lending library in Paris under the name of Shakespeare and Co. This brave woman risked what professional publishers did not wish to, she took the manuscript and handed it to the printers."); the first page of the novel itself containing but two words—"Stately, plump"—the *S* filling the entire leaf.

I put it on the basement shelf. When Friday came and I went to retrieve it, the spine and edges were all torn up. At first I thought another employee had found some other beat-up copy and swapped it. Upon closer inspection, I deduced the real culprit: mice. Often in the basement you'd see one darting around a corner. They'd been munching on *Ulysses* all week.

I decided to buy the book anyway. I can't remember why. Until now, I never once opened it. Nor am I entirely sure why I chose to write about it here. It's certainly not my rarest or most valuable book—that'd have to be the pristine first edition of *The Autobiography of Alice B. Toklas* I found for $5 at a Daytona Beach used book store while visiting a retired aunt and uncle. And compared with, say, that of the threadbare copy of *Fiesta* (the British title of *The Sun Also Rises*) I picked up studying abroad and carried with me to Paris and Pamplona, its backstory isn't very enthralling. I suppose settling on *Ulysses* as my most cherished book has to do with it fast approaching a decade since my arrival in New York and stint at the Strand—struggling to keep up with my course load and prohibited by store policy from working part time, I found a more flexible job passing hors d'oeuvres for a catering company—and my naiveté toward the city having long worn off. I know now not only when to keep my mouth shut but where to stand on subway platforms to save time transferring trains. I know to show up for a movie no less than forty-five minutes beforehand and that admission prices at the Met are merely *recommended*. I know the protocol for ordering porterhouse at Peter Luger, and that a great spot to watch the Macy's fireworks (that is, until they were moved from the East River to the Hudson) is the Long Island City piers, and at what bar to find a game of Beirut. And I know that while I'll never truly be a New Yorker—a distinction reserved for the born-and-raised—I've earned the right to call this city my home.

Believe It or Not!

―――――――――

SARAH MANGUSO

I was brought up quiet, amid strangers' debris.

When I was young, each week my parents and I visited the Wellesley (Massachusetts) Recycling and Disposal Facility. Monstrous containers held every kind of color-sorted glass, metal, paper, and earth.

Beyond the bins was a cleared lot where my parents found tables and chairs and I found board games and skis. There were stage lights, painted plaster animals, and always a pile of crutches and walkers, as if a miracle-spring bubbled nearby. Sometimes you could find jade lamps and silver plate, and only the townspeople, whose cars wore official stickers, were allowed in. It was like a country club.

Beyond the swap lot, as if an afterthought, was the place for noncompostable garbage, and beyond the garbage, up a steep hill, was a book swap housed in a lean-to—what we called the Dump Library. It was better than the local town library, a former one-room schoolhouse with a dirt basement, little money or space for new books, and a card catalog hand-typed by the obedient dead.

The Dump Library's long shelves held geography magazines and abridged encyclopedias, that core collection seasoned with law school textbooks, pharmacology references, and back issues of financial journals. There were floral- and foil-jacketed novels by improbably named women and men, and several copies apiece of curricular novellas endorsed by the old as stimulating to the young.

The rest of it was a wormhole. I brought home a thriller on whose blessed page 168 I found a man described as being *stiff as a flagpole*; I assumed this referred to his fine posture, though in the scene, inexplicably, he was lying down. I brought home a geometry notebook written in pencil in an Arabic language and a carton of letters sent from one teenaged girl at summer camp to another teenaged girl back in town. The letters contained numeric codes. The coded parts were about *making out*. (Making what out?)

The best book I ever found was a 1929 edition of Robert L. Ripley's *Believe It or Not!* bound in green cloth stamped with red ink. On the title page was an inscription in thick black fountain ink: *To Gene Cugnet with all good wishes from Rip "Believe it or Not" Feb. 27 New York 1929.*

My mother told me I should claim Gene Cugnet was my uncle, as if further personal attachment to the book were necessary to impress my friends, but I had no interest in Mr. Cugnet beyond the sound of his name, which I have known for thirty years and never thought to locate in humanity.

Who was Gene Cugnet?

From the U.S. Social Security Death Index:

SARAH MANGUSO

Gene CUGNET
Birth Date: 12 Mar 1884
Death Date: Aug 1962
Social Security Number: 017-12-3308
State or Territory Where Number Was Issued: Massachusetts
Actual Death Residence: Massachusetts

So he was forty-four, more than halfway done with his life, when he met Rip in New York City, maybe on a trip with his family. Why not? It was the Roaring Twenties.

The book didn't turn up at the dump until fifteen or twenty years later. Maybe Gene's offspring dutifully enjoyed the bound memento of their dear father's New York trip, then tired of it. Maybe the books surrounding it on the Dump Library shelf had also been Gene's. Or maybe—imagine this—the book had been brought there in 1962, right after Gene's death, then picked up by some unknown reader and enjoyed for twenty years, *then brought back to the dump a second time*. It is not improbable that the book stayed local. My parents have lived within five miles of the dump for a combined total of 168 years.

I remember almost every page of that Ripley book, from the Cyclops Girl to the Eyeless Girl to the shape of Rameses II's nose, which I found in 1998 on the face of a man in my graduate program and immediately took to bed. How could I not? He had the nose of an immortal!

I remember Rabelais's will—*I have nothing / I owe much / The rest I leave to the poor*—and I remember that the man with the shortest name in the United States of America as of 1928 was Ed Ek, of Brockton, Mass.

The book is just in the other room, but I'm showing off, writing this from memory.

> *A pound of feathers weighs more than a pound of gold.*
> *All female rulers named Jane were murdered, became insane,*
>   *or were deposed.*
> *All the names of God have four letters.*
> *There is no cork in cork legs. (The name comes from Dr. Cork*
>   *who invented them.)*
> *Red snow falls in Japan.*

Rip's beautiful ink drawings often included text at the bottom, its arrangement on the page rendering punctuation unnecessary.

> *Henry Lewis*
> *playing billiards with his nose*
>   *made a run of 46*

> *A cat*
> *adopted and*
>   *mothered*
>   *a rat*

There was the eight-year-old mother, the ninety-year-old mother, and the great-great-great-great grandmother, whose tombstone read:

> *The Mother to her daughter spake:*
>   *"Daughter," said she, "Arise!*
> *They daughter to her daughter take,*
>   *Whose daughter's daughter cries."*

Thirty years after I first read the book, I can find, in a few minutes, with the aid of telecommunicative tools, the probability that one of Mr. Cugnet's distant relatives was a woman named Marvelous Tytlandsvik of Maxim, Saskatchewan. Her surname is Norwegian, named for a town in the county of Rogaland. Page 94 of the 1903 Baedeker (8th ed.) for Norway, Sweden and Denmark reads *We next enter the Hjøsenfjord, with its wild and grand rocks, somewhat resembling the Lysefjord, and call at Tytlandsvik or Tøtlandsvik on a bay of its S. bank, and at Valde on its N. bank....* The town is known today as Totlandsvika.

I felt calmer and more myself back when all of my friends and I had each collected fewer than a hundred books of our own to read. When we spent time together, we told each other about them. Then we went home and drew a picture on a newsprint pad, or walked into the woods to look for red and orange leaves.

I remember the photo of all the Chinese people walking four abreast out to infinity, with the terrifying statistic that if they walked past a fixed point, they would never stop:

> *If all the Chinese in the world*
> *were to march 4 abreast past a given point*
> *they would never finish passing*
> *though they marched forever and ever*
> *(based on U.S. Army marching regulations)*

And I remember the cipher that begins *U O a O but I O thee, O O no O but O O me....* (*You sigh for a cipher but I sigh for thee, O sigh for no cipher but O sigh for me....*)

The ink of Rip's line drawings is dark black, fading to charcoal at the edges of the lines, and the paper is thick eggshell pulp. I never thought to take special care of the book, and I am sure that at least some of the rings on it from wet drinking glasses are marks that I left while sick at home, sipping ginger ale to calm my nervous stomach, brought on by anxiety, which often kept me home from school and was always called a *stomach ailment.*

I learned as much from that book as I learned in nearly all my years of public school, though perhaps because I had terrible attendance, something I never thought necessary to measure— unlike the longest fingernails in the world, the tardiest postal letter ever delivered, or the heaviest lemon ever grown—until graduation, at which I learned that there was such a thing as a Perfect Attendance Award and that my classmate David Robertson hadn't missed a day of school in thirteen years. Perhaps not coincidentally, he had been raised a Christian Scientist. (Believe it or not!)

Rip's antique English and archaic jokes entered my lexicon insidiously.

I have traveled in 64 countries—including Hell (Norway), and the strangest thing I saw was man.

Strange Is Man When He Seeks After His Gods. Therefore the strangest places on earth are the holiest. And the strangest and most remarkable city in the world is the holy city of Benares on the muddy arm of the Ganges, India's holy river. . . .

Rip met and sketched an Indian juggler who was able to lift a sack filled with poisonous snakes by suction cups attached to his eyeballs. The ragged man on the bed of nails is hardly impressive next to the drawing of the even more ragged man who had been a galley slave for one hundred years and a day. The most dated believe-it-or-nots were the most believable. So what if *Frau C. Worth, owner of a large apartment house in Berlin, did not collect any rents from her tenants for twenty years*? So what if, at the age of eleven, Sidis (his first names, *William James*, were superfluous in 1929) *matriculated in Harvard and astounded his professors by discussing the fourth dimension*?

Ripley was a cartoonist, entrepreneur, and amateur anthropologist. He wrote about hundred-pound pumpkins with the same blithe wonder as he described the Kewawngdu, the Giraffe women of Burma. According to the reference I am now reading, in 1929, the year he signed my book, he published the following in his long-running syndicated series of newspaper cartoons: *Believe it or not, America has no national anthem.* Two years later, President Hoover signed a law designating "The Star-Spangled Banner" as the national anthem of the United States.

Rip also ran a chain of Odditorium museums, hosted a radio program and then, in 1949, a television program. Other shows on the air in 1949 included *Missus Goes a Shopping, Foodini the Great, Champagne and Orchids,* and *The Family Genius.* Rip died on set, during the filming of the thirteenth episode. Before his death, he had been voted the most popular man in America by the *New York Times.*

It is tempting to conclude that children should be given only the cast-offs of the dead to read, with no duplicate copies within a hundred miles, but I can't know what it was like to be the other kind of child, and there is no moral.

William Trevor:
The Collected Stories

VICTORIA PATTERSON

I was about to graduate from the MFA program in Creative Writing at UC Riverside—about to turn in my thesis—and every time
I drove to school from South Pasadena, I'd pass an ominous
bright yellow billboard on the 210 East Freeway, with the nu-
merals 6-6-06 in bold black, and beneath them—in the same
black lettering—the admonition: YOU'VE BEEN WARNED. For
the last few weeks, in conjunction with the end of my two-year
higher education respite from the real world, and in anticipation
of my dreaded reentry, I'd been obsessing on death. I felt a slight
resentment at the billboard, and at myself for letting it work its
creepy voodoo on me at all. Exhausted mentally and physically
and emotionally, not sleeping well at night, I'd look at people—
whether at the grocery store or a party or even in the cars next to
me on the freeway—and involuntarily recognize that they'd soon
be dead. We'd all be dead. I couldn't shake the death thoughts.

My youngest son, in kindergarten at the time, seemed to be in
emotional synchronicity with me. One night we watched the
movie *Ice Age* and, triggered by the death of the wooly mam-
moth's wife and daughter, he got very sad and weepy. He didn't
want people and animals and things to die, he said, because then

he'd miss them—the way he missed his great-grandpa Robert and our beloved dog, Wahine. Why did they have to die? What did it all mean? Why are we here? With the tears beginning to slide down his cheeks, he said, "I don't want you to die, Mommy. I don't want you to die!"

"You're six," I wanted to say, "too young for existential angst." Instead, I lay with him in his bed, comforting him, stroking his back, and I thought about that crazy billboard, wondering who'd funded it, and why they'd felt it necessary to spend that amount of money to bully people into what seemed to me an Armageddon-themed submission to God based on the supposed sign of the devil. When my son fell asleep, I went to my computer and a Google search revealed that the billboard was actually a movie promotion for the slated release of the remake of *The Omen*. Capitalizing on people's fears and using religious mania as a marketing tool, I decided, might possibly be worse than religious mania itself.

I'd been exchanging e-mails with Dwight Yates, a lecturer in Creative Writing at UC Riverside whose writing and taste in literature I admired. In an e-mail I read that night he casually mentioned his fondness for the Irish writer William Trevor. One of the best parts of graduate school was filling in the gaps of my reading history with professor recommendations, and I decided that the following day—6-6-06—instead of further indulging in morbidity, I'd take a counterintuitive positive action and purchase a book: a sort of commitment to my reading life and writing life—to life itself—no matter what happened beyond graduate school.

In the morning, my two sons and I went to Vroman's Bookstore in Pasadena, and I came upon *William Trevor: The Collected Stories*, a whopping 1,261-page paperback with a black-and-white headshot of Mr. Trevor on the cover, wearing a tweed hat similar to one that I owned. I'm not one to fall sway to author photographs, because they don't bespeak the quality of the work and can be off-putting or deceiving. If I had been influenced by Raymond Carver looking astute and angry in Marion Ettlinger's well-known photograph of him, or Ernest Hemingway in his gigantic turtleneck, sad and arrogant with his gaze cast to the side and upward in an ironically angelic pose, I might never have read their work. But this time I was taken in. Mr. Trevor's face was heavily and beautifully wrinkled, his ears were large and fleshy, and he barely smiled. He stared right at me—kind, wise, mischievous, patient—as if saying, "There's so much to read and know and write and learn, and you're just at the beginning."

The weight of the book was also an attraction: it portended commitment. So, along with a selection of Captain Underpants books chosen by my kids, I made our purchase.

I appreciated holding *William Trevor: The Collected Stories*— eighty-five stories written over thirty years—in my hands; opening the book and smelling the woodsy-glue pages; the tactile feel of turning a page—the soft *shhh* as my finger slid it, and then the flap of it as it turned and settled with the previous page. And I could take a pen and underline passages or star them and anoint them with my own personal exclamation marks at the margins, and my own comments: *How did he do that? Why does it make me feel sad here? Look at how he introduces her to the reader.*

On a screen, I don't get the sense of accumulation that I do with a physical book: the weight of the pages moving from my right hand to my left hand, a history building and adding on itself. On a screen, pages disappear. For me, e-books are like ghosts of books. They're not here.

Soon, *William Trevor: The Collected Stories* was with me in the passenger seat when I drove. *William Trevor: The Collected Stories* went to my kids' swimming lessons. *William Trevor: The Collected Stories* went to the park, to baseball games, to pool parties. William Trevor went with us everywhere that summer.

"That's a big book you got there," I heard often.

Midway through the book, I wrote an e-mail to Dwight Yates with the subject heading: I LOVE WILLIAM TREVOR.

Just a quick hello to tell you that I can't stop reading William Trevor. I'm about halfway through and it's all I want to read. I'm taking notes on each story on how he does this or that—underlining passages. Thanks so much for alerting me. He's a wonderful writer. Some of his stories make me weep. Others make me feel like I've been punched. He's not writing the same story over again, dressing it up different, as can happen. He has such a grand scope, dealing with pain and defeat, the inevitability of fate as accorded by actions both small and large, and they're told with unflinching details. The range of knowledge and depth of feeling, the profundity and tenderness, and the steady underlying comedic heartbeat deeply impress me.

The book became a talisman for me. I took it with me to the coffee shops or the houses where I wrote, so that, worst-case scenario, if I had trouble writing, I could read and be inspired. But simply with the book near me—within touching distance, so that I could take breaks and flip through its many pages, or stare beseechingly at Mr. Trevor's face—two stories flowed near effortlessly from me that summer, as if in a dream. Instead of taking years to write, as my stories usually do, they came within months, successively, miraculously.

The pages of the book became stain-filled—coffee, water, a smear of sun block. Passages were underlined in red, black, purple, and blue ink. From a large splash at my youngest son's swimming lesson that had left a section of the book sopping wet, a full quarter of the pages curled jauntily upward when they dried, as if they'd been released from a hair roller.

Four years later, pages creased, even more pen-marked, and with a torn cover, *William Trevor: The Collected Stories* is still with me whenever and wherever I write. The book is floppy now, because the glue at the spine is giving out, and the pages are beginning to have that faded yellow-on-the-outside-whiter-on-the-inside look that older books sometimes get. When I press my face inside the book, it still smells good. From a beach trip with my sons, the last hundred or so pages are thickly rippled, having endured a very wet towel being placed over the book—opened somewhere near one of my favorite stories, "In Love with Ariadne"—for an hour or more before the offense was discovered and remedied. Like the arms of a dead and drying starfish, all corners of the book curl outward now, not just the section from my youngest son's swimming lesson.

His anxieties about death are not gone—they ebb and wane, as do mine. Yet we understand that books—especially a great book like *William Trevor: The Collected Stories*—have the affirming capability of shrinking anxieties, not by ignoring fears and doubts or making light of death, or even by appeasing uncertainties, but by witnessing and connecting, letting us know that we're not alone.

The Once and Future King

KAREN JOY FOWLER

When I was about seventeen years old, a noted professor of literature from the University of Sussex came to dinner at our home in Palo Alto. His name was Reginald Mutter. My older brother had met him as an exchange student in Sussex the previous year. I don't remember why Professor Mutter was in the States—perhaps he was doing something at Stanford, perhaps he was merely on vacation. In any case, he came to eat with us and to borrow our car for the duration of his visit. My parents liked to gather in traveling faculty. Our dinner table was often thick with them.

I am a member in good standing of a *very* bookish family and on this particular evening we talked mostly about books. I told Professor Mutter how much I liked Tolkien's *The Lord of the Rings*, but not so much Lewis's *The Lion, the Witch, and the Wardrobe* and he told me about the Inklings, the Oxford literary group to which both men had belonged. We talked about Austen and the troubling protagonists of *Mansfield Park*. We talked about Fielding, whom I hadn't read. We talked about the Brontës. Professor Mutter seemed to share most of my enthusiasms. Buoyed by this, I brought up *The Wind in the Willows*.

My father and I had a long-running feud about *The Wind and the Willows*. He'd attempted to read it once, found it slow going, and quit. If a book didn't engage him in the first thirty pages, he said, then it was a bad book. I was willing to concede that the first thirty pages were sleepy. I was not willing to concede it was a bad book. In fact, I loved it with all my heart. But our argument had less to do with the merits of *The Wind and the Willows* and more with the principle that a book beloved by so many could be summarily dismissed as bad by someone who hadn't read very much of it. I felt certain Professor Mutter was smart enough to see how unfair my dad was being.

Professor Mutter's response was to quote A. A. Milne, who'd said that one did not argue about *The Wind in the Willows*. A young man gave it to the woman he loved and, if she didn't care for it, broke off the engagement. Professor Mutter was too polite to quote the part that comes later, the part I found afterwards, where Milne says that liking the book is a test of character. But I could read between the lines: Professor Mutter agreed with me and so did *A. A. Milne*! Dad was thoroughly routed.

I told Professor Mutter that T. H. White's *The Once and Future King* was my favorite book. Dad and I also disagreed about it, but since he didn't contend it was a bad book, this argument was less gut-wrenching. At seventeen, I didn't like my father much. It shames me to say so. I had my reasons and some of them were good reasons, but none of them was good enough.

He is, without question, the person who influenced me most as a writer. It embarrasses me how often I write about him. Sometimes I know I'm doing so. Sometimes I realize it only later. Sometimes I don't realize it and my brother has to point it out to me. *Look there. Dad, again.*

My father was the person who taught me how to throw a ball and how to fly-fish. He read me *Mary Poppins* and also *The Iliad*. He gave me the poetry of Emily Dickinson and also García Lorca. When I was little he used to read me Noyes's "The Highwayman," because it made me cry, which he bizarrely seemed to think meant I wished to hear it again. When we lived in Indiana, he was Merlin to my Wart and taught me my place in the natural world. I mean that in the big ways, but also the small. He could identify every bird and the tree it was in, and so, as a result, could I. He showed me the constellations, how to crack open a geode to find the Fabergé egg–like world inside, and how to identify poison ivy.

We stopped getting along about the time I turned eleven. This was also the year we moved from Indiana to California, the year he left the Psychology Department at Indiana University for a corporate job with Encyclopedia Britannica Films. It's easy to think that these things damaged our relationship; we were both so unhappy then, each of us in a place we didn't belong. But then, eleven is, for so many girls, the age at which everything goes wrong.

My father hadn't had much of a father himself and so had to make the whole thing up from scratch. He was more comfortable as a college professor than as a dad. He had a study in the back of the house with a large blackboard and if he ever had something difficult to talk to me about, or, as was less frequent, I had something I wanted to say to him, he'd insist on going into that room. He would stand, chalk in hand, at that blackboard while we talked. I would sit. I suspect he would have liked me to be taking notes.

I'd found *The Once and Future King* while panning in the public library. Because I'd found it on my own and not with my father's guidance, he couldn't completely approve. I was perhaps fourteen years old when I first read it. It launched me on an Arthurian quest from which I have never come home.

When I'd finished *The Once and Future King*, Dad sent me to a different part of the library, to a different book, one he felt had actual archaeological integrity. This book may have been Henry Treece's *The Green Man*, but it may not have been. (Just as I may or may not have been fourteen years old at the time. There is a reason I don't write memoir.) I read this other book and thought it was okay. I returned it to the library and checked out *The Once and Future King* again.

The only thing that can be said against rereading is that it does retard your overall progress through the canon. In every other way, its pleasures surpass even those of reading something for the first time. I checked *The Once and Future King* out of the library many times over the next few years, and it was clear I intended to keep on doing so.

Eventually Dad read it, too. I think he finished it, but am not sure. He thought it was pretty good. He just didn't like all the silliness in the second part—all the bits concerning Grummore, Palomides, and the psychoanalysis of the Questing Beast. A terrible failure of taste, my father said.

In some corner of my mind, I must have already known I would be a writer. I look at my past and see an unblemished record of cutting the writer some slack. Who cares if the beginning is slow? Who cares if some of the jokes fall flat as a vaudeville act? Even at fourteen, I could see that, in just those places my father identified, T. H. White was trying to be funny and failing. My father was absolutely right.

But I didn't then (and don't now) wish those parts gone. There was something so intimate in that very failure. That White would trust me enough to show me not only his best side but also his most tasteless! Perhaps the book did suffer as a result, but White and I were all the closer for it. I feel this way about many of the flawed books I've come to love. The warts are where you see the writer. Don't edit out the warts.

If my father is the person who most influenced my writing, *The Once and Future King* is the book. Sometimes, shockingly, I'll be looking at it again and find an image I've used in my own work, a thought I'd honestly thought was mine. I've read it so often, over so many years, that it's become a part of me.

It was my defense—my portcullis, if you will—when I began to write myself and to hear in workshops a lot of talk about rules I hadn't known, contracts with the reader I'd unwittingly violated. But whenever there was a thing I was told I couldn't do, nine times out of ten White had already done it.

So I knew there was no real need to pick a genre, learn its conventions, and write sedately from within it. White swings from magic to history to fantasy to science fiction to satire to realism to myth. His historical research is prodigious, yet he never hesitates to throw a juicy anachronism into the pot. It helps to have a main character living backwards in time. There are talking animals. God appears as the dazzle on a shield. Football hooligans are taken sternly to task. Guenever is drawn with a perspicacious sympathy I will, in future readings, seldom see again.

The mood is sometimes lighthearted and hilarious, but just as often heartbreaking. My favorite part is the third section: "The Ill-Made Knight." White's Lancelot, struggling throughout against his own self-loathing, is my most beloved character. Years later, another writer told me that section was the autobiographical one—that it mirrored White's own struggle against his homosexuality. I don't know if that's true. I do know I find the pages devoted to Lancelot profoundly moving. (How irritated I was to find, in the musical version, that Lancelot had become a blowhard with a pretty face. The first in an ongoing saga of adaptational betrayals.)

There is likewise no consistency in White's tone or voice. He is poetic one minute and dryly academic the next. He uses the narrative strategy I tend toward myself (and I'm sure he's the reason I lean that way): lots of helpful (and bossy) intrusion, lots of direct address, *lots* of digression. He doesn't hesitate to put the action on pause so as to explain the rules of tilting and why it is a bit like scuba diving and a bit like American football, or to lecture on natural history, or to comment on earlier texts. "There is no need to give a long description of the tourney," White says at one point. "Malory gives it."

I doubt I said any of this during our dinner with Professor Mutter. I don't remember much of what I did say. I do remember that my father was uncharacteristically quiet. Possibly he knew, for once, that he was not the expert at the table, but that doesn't sound much like my dad. I believe instead that he could see that Professor Mutter was enjoying my enthusiasm. I believe Dad was quiet because he was proud of me.

After he returned to England, Professor Mutter sent me T. H. White's children's book, *Mistress Masham's Repose*. "I know you're not too old for this," he wrote in the accompanying note. "Because I'm not too old for it." Meanwhile, my father had bought me my very own copy of *The Once and Future King*. A dinner party that nets you two novels is a very good dinner party.

Dad had inscribed the book with a poem:

FOR KAREN,
  Arthur, King,
    With strength + grace,
  A knight of lance
    And sword + mace,
  A queenly girl
    Who loved them both,
  A bastard son,
    Reared in wroth,

  This the stuff
    For Merlin's mold,
  This the tale,
    Not fully told,

For who of us
  Can ever know
The errant play
  Beneath the show?

This gift of affirmation didn't mark any big change in our relationship, at least not quickly enough for him to enjoy it. I never got to fix things with him, be more generous, more appreciative. My father died when I was twenty-three. I'm sure this is why I keep writing about him.

If I lived backwards in time, here are some of the things I'd have told him:

I'd have told him I would become a writer, which he didn't live to see. I have his own unpublished novel, a revisionist look at Judas similar in concept to the one in Kazantzakis's *The Last Temptation of Christ*. I remember how crushed Dad was when he read that book.

I'd have told him that the last four lines of the poem he would someday give me—the part beginning with "For who of us can ever know"—are as succinct a summation of what I'm about when I write as anything I could concoct. I'm always looking for the untold story. The part you don't know yet. The errant play. Nicely put, Dad.

I'd have told him that the fact that he signed the poem "Clete," his first name, on a gift to his daughter, is something I still ponder with affectionate befuddlement.

And I'd have told him that I still reread *The Once and Future King*. But far more often, I'd have told him, I take the book from the shelf and open it just to look at your handwriting on the flyleaf.

The Carpetbaggers

RABIH ALAMEDDINE

I was raised in the desert of Kuwait in the 1960s, a time when it was a desert in every sense of the word: sand, heat, and technology's greatest gift, air-conditioning. There was nothing to do. We were Lebanese expats, strangers in a barren land.

I read.

I read everything in sight, anything within reach. I started out with comic books, of course. I believe I began before being able to put letters together to form words, let alone words to form sentences. Superman and Batman, Wonder Woman and the Justice League, Archie and Jughead, Asterix and Obelix, Casper and Richie Rich, Tintin and Lulu and Lotta, Lucky Luke and Baby Huey. I graduated to Enid Blyton books: the Famous Five and the Secret Seven. As a child I knew more about how to serve tea in the afternoon than how to converse with Kuwaiti kids.

A story: I was about seven. I was in the living room reading, probably the Secret Seven series. My mother yelled my name. She was in her bedroom. She spoke slowly, in a tone used whenever she wanted to be exquisitely understood.

"Call your father at work right now. Tell him to bring a doctor right away. I'm fainting. It's an emergency."

I did as instructed. On the phone my nervous father asked me how my mother was, and I replied, "She's in the room, probably fainting."

He arrived not ten minutes later, though his place of work was at least twenty-five minutes away. He walked into the living room and I was sitting in his chair reading. Shocked, he asked me where my mother was. I replied she was in her room. I grew slightly nervous. I was reading in my father's chair since it had the best light. If my father didn't return to work, he'd reclaim it and I'd have to use another. Our Egyptian neighbor, a doctor, rushed through the door. I pointed to the bedroom. An hour later, my father came out of the room and lectured me. I shouldn't have left my mother alone. She had fainted, hitting her vanity as she fell and a small piece of jutting aluminum had stabbed her on the side. She woke up, bleeding. That was when she called me in. Then she fainted once more after I left. My mother had told me only to call my father. I did that. She didn't say she needed me. My book did, so I'd returned to it.

My mother understood, for she, too, was a reader. She would read in one corner of the living room, and I in another, both of us in antipodal armchairs, feet tucked under butts, books held up at eye level, lost in another world, a world richer than Kuwait's oil-laden desert.

It wasn't long before I began to pick up her books. At the time she read mostly bestsellers, the only books easily found in expat bookstores. Frederick Forsyth, John le Carré, James Michener, Jacqueline Susann (Sparkle, Neely, sparkle!), and . . . and . . . wait for it . . . Harold Robbins.

My dear Harold was the writer who captured my heart toward the end of my preteens. His is a much-maligned oeuvre, whose value to sexually deprived young boys is underappreciated. The sweeping emotional dramas, the grand betrayals, the triumph of good, and delightful sentences like "She stroked his penis with two fingers" were perfect reading when I was twelve.

Here's a delightful fact: Let any used Harold Robbins book fall open to the creased parts, you'll find all the dirty bits. Saves time. This spine-drop technique works anywhere in the world. I even tried it on a Robbins book in a house in Chengdu, China. Works every time.

The book that snared me was *The Carpetbaggers.* I remember being unable to put it down. I had left Kuwait. Summer in the mountains of Lebanon, I was ensconced on a couch, and my cousins, all girls, all older than I, all taller teenagers, insisted that I accompany them on a walk. Fresh air and all that. They dragged me out. Chatting, giggling, strolling along the mountain road. I lagged behind a few steps, until I was able to open the pocket book. I began to read as I walked. A large truck was parked on the side of the road. Lost in the sweeping vengeful world of *The Carpetbaggers* I walked under that truck and slammed my head against one of its brake lights. My cousins weren't able to stop giggling for a week.

I had another cousin, three years older than I, whom I'd desperately looked up to. I spoke to her about my love.

"I must read that book of yours," she said, and she did.

I was disappointed, but mostly shocked, that she wasn't crazy about it, not even a little.

"What about the story? What about the adventure?"

"Such a story," she said gently, returning the dog-eared copy, "I'd rather see in a movie. I like my books a bit different."

Fortunately, or unfortunately, infatuations fade, rather quickly, too. It took less than a year to lose mine with Robbins. In those days I fell in and out of love with writers quicker than Byron. I began to read books that were a bit different. I still read everything in sight for quite a while, but Robbins began to sound childish to my adolescent ears. At thirteen, I considered *The Carpetbaggers* puerile, and I took that as proof that I had finally become a man.

My bookshelves smiled with new weights and colors. Rejected though it might have felt, that faded, lightweight pocket book still found a place between my new loves.

The civil war started in 1975, when I was fifteen. I was shipped to boarding school in England and after that to UCLA. My family didn't leave Lebanon. I returned regularly during those years, once every six months or so. Coward though I am, I braved the war, slept in my room in our house in the mountains, among my books. I moved back to Lebanon after graduating at the end of 1981, but the Israelis invaded a few months later, upping the war's ante, and I returned to America.

My family's house in the mountains, my father's dream house that he'd built, had survived seven years of the civil war. With the open involvement of the Israelis, and the Americans soon after, my parents knew that the house and our village were no longer safe. My mother packed the valuables, the sentimental and the expensive, and shut down the house. She packed my albums, hundreds of them, and most of my books.

She saved my books. In my bookshelf in San Francisco, I have a few hardcovers from those days: Iris Murdoch's *The Sea, the Sea* and *Henry and Cato*, John Fowles's *The Magus* and *Daniel Martin*, *The Complete Works of William Shakespeare*, and the book that I treasure most, Naipaul's *A House for Mr. Biswas*. She didn't save any of the pocket books, definitely not *The Carpetbaggers*.

In the summer of 1982 the American battleship *New Jersey* sent a sixteen-inch shell through the roof of our house. The structure remained standing—roofless and badly charred, but standing. My family didn't have the heart to inspect the house for four years—neither the heart nor the willingness to encounter the various armies and militias that had camped in it after the shelling. The Israelis and the Syrians, the Druze and Christian and Muslim militias all were guests in our house at different times.

In the summer of 1988, my father took me up to look at the remains of our home, what was once his pride and joy. He'd been to the house before that visit and joked that it was in better shape than most of the Roman ruins in the country. Political and obscene graffiti covered the half-torn walls. There was no ceiling and surprisingly no floor: the parquet, the stone, the marble, all looted. Toilets, faucets, wiring, pipes, bathtubs, furniture, bookshelves, everything was gone. The house smelled of decay, cordite, and urine. My room, once red, was now blood gray.

But in one of the corners of the room lay the old copy of *The Carpetbaggers*. It no longer had a cover, and some of the pages were missing, although I didn't check which ones. Ragged, it barely hung together. It was the only thing in the room that wasn't stolen. I couldn't tell how many fighters had read it. I didn't take it. I didn't even pick it up off the floor. I left it there.

I don't know. I thought it was too dirty or something. I never saw it again.

Years later, I would begin to write. I no longer had the unfettered time to read everything in sight. My tastes narrowed even more. My close friends consider me a literary snob.

I had a dinner party not too long ago. One of those friends arrived bearing a gift. He intended it as camp, to make fun of me a bit, to pinprick my pretensions. Not knowing anything about my history with the book, he'd found an early-edition hardcover of *The Carpetbaggers* at a garage sale for one whole dollar, a used copy, clean and crisp. He bought it for me as a joke. He was stunned when I burst into tears upon receiving it.

As I write this in my study, the book sits before me in one of my bookshelves. All I have to do is turn my eyes slightly right of the computer screen, and I can see it, at home between Alain Robbe-Grillet and Marilynne Robinson.

The New Professional Chef, Fifth Edition

MICHAEL RUHLMAN

Penurious writer that I was, I took what would become the most important book of my life out of the Shaker Heights Public Library rather than purchase the fifty-dollar behemoth. It was the summer of 1995. I was nearly thirty-three years old, with a wife and newborn daughter, casting about for a second nonfiction book project. I'd just sent off the manuscript of my first book, about a boys school, and we were subsisting on the last of the advance until I could come up with a valid proposal for another.

The book—a big green anchor weighing more than six pounds—was *The New Professional Chef, Fifth Edition*, the official textbook of the Culinary Institute of America, the most prominent cooking school in the country, located in New York's Hudson Valley. I'd had all kinds of book proposal ideas, few of them worth pursuing according to my agent, except for this one: the notion of actually going to this school and writing about what happens inside it from the vantage point of a student. I'd written a letter to the CIA's president, Ferdinand Metz, introducing myself and offering to spend a year there in order to write a book about learning to cook professionally (a deal I presumed he was already rubbing his hands together over, readying the red carpet for the writer who would give unprecedented coverage of his chef school). While I waited for his response, I read much of the book, but it was text heavy, with a lot of unappealing and inscrutable and downright unhelpful photographs (three different plates of flour cooked with butter to different colors, from pale to brown; shots of pots and pans that were obviously pots and pans) as well as illustrations of common vegetables (ah, so *that's* a red bell pepper).

A few weeks after returning it to the library I received my own copy in the mail—an unexpected birthday present from my mother's boyfriend, an avid cook. I hadn't asked for it; I didn't know if I'd get my book project off the ground, and if I didn't, I wouldn't need another leaden tour through its incomprehensible pages. But there it was, a book I was meant to own.

This volume would not be the most impenetrable text I'd delve into for a book project. Several years later, I'd attempt to fathom congenital heart disease and its surgical repair. True, there were some lavish shots of *pâtés en terrine* and other finished dishes that were more comprehensible and pleasant to behold than diagrams of Hypoplastic Left Heart Syndrome. And certainly the medical textbook did not have recipes for jambalaya and chocolate mousse to spark the imagination. But there was something similarly technical and forbidding in this cookbook, even in the recipes, page after page of them with no pictures and no explanatory notes to let you know what you were about to get yourself into, and most of them created to serve upwards of twenty or thirty people or yield a gallon of sauce.

I read it again, this time able to underline significant sentences, guesses as to what may or may not be important. I'd already figured out that recipes weren't what cooking was all about, that recipes were a dime a dozen (and soon, thanks to the Internet, a penny per thousand), that real cooking required something more ineffable than a quart of stock, two sliced onions, two carrots, a quarter cup of tomato paste, and a *sachet d'epices* (whatever the heck that was—ah, thank goodness for the brief but useful glossary: "'Bag of spices.' Aromatic ingredients, encased in cheesecloth, that are used to flavor stocks and other liquids. A standard sachet contains parsley stems, cracked peppercorns, dried thyme and a bay leaf"). I did sense something revealing in the structure of the book, however. Most cookbooks I owned were organized by courses, or categories of food—appetizers, soups and salads, chicken, beef, dessert. This one was much different. After preliminary chapters on kitchen protocol, sanitation, ingredients, something called "Meat Fabrication," it then organized itself by oddly termed cooking methods such as "Dry-Heat Cooking with Fats and Oils" and "Charcuterie and Garde Manger."

There was also a brief foreword—four paragraphs on a single large page—written by Mr. Metz, who continued to ignore what I thought to be a mutually beneficial request. (After several phone calls, I learned that he'd passed my letter on to someone else; my query didn't require his attention, let alone his response.) Yet his foreword opened with the very words that had motivated me in my quest to worm my way into his school in the first place: "There is a widespread misconception about how one becomes a chef," he began. Well, yes! I thought. Precisely the problem I'd like to address in my book that should take place at your school! Where are the rose petals, Mr. Metz?

Becoming a chef was more than rote memorizing of recipes, he continued. There were no magic tools or ingredients in the professional restaurant kitchen. There were instead basic techniques that one sought to grasp, asking questions along the way throughout one's career as one strove for technical mastery that would ultimately bestow on the serious student of cooking "the profound sensibility that allows him or her to distinguish the substantial from the trivial."

"As we continue to learn," Metz concluded, "we are brought at last to the realization that it is simplicity, in cooking as in all arts, that demands the greatest artistry and offers the greatest rewards."

The elegance of this foreword intensified both my desire and my frustration. As July turned to August and August became September, my lack of having spoken with anyone who could clear my way into the school became stress producing in that I had accepted an advance from my publisher against the future royalties of this book that I now didn't know if I'd be able even to begin. I'd have no way of paying it back if this school remained as impenetrable as the massive cooking textbook I'd given up trying to understand.

In October, the CIA's senior vice president found time to meet with me, but we parted company that day with no actual agreement that they would let me in. Meanwhile, my wife had found a garage apartment twenty-five miles north of the school in Tivoli, New York, so that we could increase the rate at which we were burning through the book advance.

Perhaps sensing by then that I was not going away, the Culinary Institute of America at last gave in to my request, and arranged for me to begin "Skill Development I" on the third Tuesday in January 1996. I brought to class a knife kit and a leather shoulder briefcase containing the very heavy *New Pro Chef*, as it was referred to. It was to this book that my chef instructor would ask us to turn during our evening lecture. Brown sauce, *sauce Espagnole*, a classic mother sauce with far-reaching implications—we would be making only a fraction of the recipe in the book, he said, and gave us the proportions we would prepare for evaluation. He revised the quantities of wine and mustard and shallot in the *Espagnole*-based *sauce Robert*, a lesson in derivative sauces. My notes and the revised quantities suggested by Chef Pardus—a half cup, down from a pint—remain fossilized evidence of my pre-cooking self.

I would change in that kitchen, K-8—I had to. Learning to cook professionally changes you from within; it forces you to think and act more efficiently, to be more organized, to refuse to say no to challenges, to understand your limits, which we found kept extending the more Chef Pardus pushed us. These changes weren't visible; they happened on the inside. Meaning I couldn't write about them from the vantage point of an observer. I had to learn to cook for real.

And so I did. And when it was time for me to go, nine months after first setting foot in K-8, it was clear that I had indeed changed, not only because I could now work a hot line but because I could write a book in four months. That's how fast I finished *The Making of a Chef: Mastering Heat at the Culinary Institute of America*, because that's when we would be broke and needing the last of the advance from my publisher. It was the same as if service were in four hours. I was going to be ready for service—because, well, you just were. Not being ready wasn't an option, unless you wanted to get your ass handed to you every night of the week.

What I'd learned in order to write that book and the changes the process had wrought in me paved the way for what would become the main work of my career: writing about food and the work of professional cooking; working with some of the best chefs in the world on their books and in their kitchens; writing more books of my own, books ultimately that were not about recipes but about story and about technique, much as that cooking textbook had taught me to organize the ideas of cooking, stocks and sauté and roast, not appetizer, main course, and dessert.

I at last understood this behemoth text that had been part of my life since the summer of 1995. I saw why it had been organized as it was, it now made sense to me, it had opened up to me. In the years since, I've again and again returned to my *New Pro Chef, Fifth Edition* for basic technique and for standard ratios, even though I own editions seven, eight, and nine. I had been one person when this very heavy construction of cardboard and binding and paper came into my life and now I am a completely different person and this is the book that stands smack in the middle of the divide of who I was and who I am.

Mythology

SIGRID NUNEZ

Although my mother loved to read, there were not many books in our house. Among her small collection was *Mythology*, by Edith Hamilton, the American classicist, born in 1867, whose life as a writer did not begin until she had retired from her profession as an educator (twenty-six years as head of the Bryn Mawr Preparatory School in Baltimore, Maryland), and who did not publish her first book (*The Greek Way*, 1930) until she was sixty-three. There was a time in my youth when I could imagine myself into a life such as Miss Hamilton's: I speak not of the bestselling author but of the dedicated spinster schoolmistress.

Mythology was first published in 1942, with illustrations by Steele Savage, whose unlikely and alarming name delighted me far more than his old-fashioned line drawings. Although it includes a final, brief chapter on Norse mythology, the rest of the book, more than three hundred pages, is devoted to the gods and heroes and royal houses of the Greeks. No surprise that my mother owned a copy. She was a great fan of mythology, classical and Norse, and very knowledgeable about both. And from its first appearance, *Mythology* was a famous and hugely popular book; it would come to be called "the classic of classics" and remains required reading in many schools today.

The book was small, a mass-market pocket book probably printed sometime in the '50s or early '60s. The cover was blue and gold with black lettering and an image of Perseus based on Benvenuto Cellini's famous bronze sculpture. Like so many of the mythological characters, human and divine—or, like Perseus himself, mixed (his father was Zeus, his mother the mortal but royal Danaë)—he is beautiful. Naked except for a pair of winged sandals and a winged cap, nobly formed, he stands with feet close together and one knee bent, a pose both elegant and incredibly sexy. In one hand he holds a sword, and, in the other, aloft, the snake-haired head of the Gorgon Medusa, whom he has just slain: an image of beauty and horror. The myth of Perseus— beautiful, horrifying—was one of the best parts of the book.

In those (better) days, when even a very famous author might remain invisible, I had no way of knowing what Hamilton looked like, but I remember that, for a while, she so resembled my mental picture of Miss Havisham that the two might have been sisters.

How old was I when I first read *Mythology*? I think around eleven or twelve. It was a natural step from the fairy tales that had been some of my favorite reading before. The book could just as well have been called *Everything You Wanted to Know*. How the world came into being; who rules heaven, earth, and hell; the origins of seasons, stars, waters, winds; why night follows day; where dreams come from; what makes a person fall in love; where we go when we die—they had it all figured out, the Greeks. And every explanation was rational in the Greek way, and beautiful in the Greek way.

By this time, I was familiar with Bible stories, and I had read other creation stories as well as various legends and fables about supernatural beings and shape-shifters and magical transformations. But I don't remember any of those affecting me quite the same way as Hamilton's myths: I could not get enough of them. (Except for that last chapter. Until much later, when I became interested in the music of Wagner, the Norse world—a joyless place "over which," as Hamilton writes, "hangs the threat of an inevitable doom," and in which the only good was a fierce and agonizing heroism—bored me to death.)

It was Hamilton's intention not only to anthologize the myths, telling them in her own words (which she does with admirable clarity), but also to give the reader something about their origins and meanings and variants, which she skillfully accomplishes without getting in the way of the stories themselves. Although she wanted above all for readers to be entertained, as she writes in a foreword, she hoped also to teach them something about the ancient writers who were her sources, and from whom she quotes frequently throughout the book. And for this reader, *Mythology* did just that, providing my first look into Homer, and the other two great Greek poets, Hesiod and Pindar; my introduction to the three great tragedians, Aeschylus, Sophocles, and Euripides; and to the Roman poets Virgil and Ovid, although Hamilton says she tried to avoid Ovid whenever possible because, though a wonderful writer, he did not believe, as the Greeks did, in the myths he was writing and often presented them frivolously.

It was in Hamilton that I first got to know them: Perseus and his even mightier descendant Hercules, Apollo and Dionysus, Oedipus and Orestes and Clytemnestra and Medea, Achilles and Odysseus, gray-eyed Athena and golden Aphrodite and Hector, tamer of horses. Horses: another girlhood passion of mine—and there could hardly be a horse more marvelous than Pegasus, who sprang from the blood of Medusa when beheaded by Perseus, and who later became the steed of Bellerophon, another "bold and beautiful young man" and slayer of that other monster, the Chimaera. How characters were related to one another, and how the various myths were intertwined, was not the least of the reasons I found them so engrossing.

I once heard Salman Rushdie give a talk in which he said that he had begun to think twice about using classical allusions in his writing, because he feared that most readers today wouldn't get them. This reminded me of something I'd read in Mary Mc-Carthy's preface to her first memoir, *Memories of a Catholic Girlhood*. Although she was to lapse from the faith as soon as she left parochial school, McCarthy would always be glad to have been born and raised a Catholic, she said, for certain practical reasons, among them the help this upbringing would turn out to be for an understanding of art and poetry and world history and the history of ideas. "Having to learn a little theology as an adult in order to understand a poem of Donne or Crashaw," she wrote, "is like being taught the Bible as Great Literature in a college humanities course: it does not stick to the ribs." The same could be said about a knowledge of mythology—and for the enormous help it has given me in my own understanding of art and literature and the development of Western culture, I feel very lucky indeed to have devoured the Greek myths at an age when there was still a chance that they'd stick to my ribs. (For those less lucky, there exists, among other resources, *Mythology for Dummies*, which comes with the guarantee that it "demystifies mythologies from all over the globe"—a little like promising to teach you Shakespeare's sonnets by de-poeticizing them.)

Different from other books read in childhood, *Mythology* was not one to be put away with childish things. I took it with me when I went away to college, a book no longer only to be reread for pleasure but an important reference. I'm sure I must have taken other books with me as well, but whatever they were I did not hold on to them, and so *Mythology* became, by many years, the oldest book I owned. In fact, except for a few photographs, it was probably my oldest possession (I am neither sentimental nor acquisitive nor a hoarder; it has always suited me best to accumulate as little stuff as possible).

After college, after graduate school, the book made many moves with me. Each time I unpacked it I found it a little more tattered. The paper darkened and turned brittle, and when the cover began to fall off I used a piece of masking tape to stick it to the spine. For years the book was a familiar beige stripe on the shelf between Bulfinch and Robert Graves. When the spine became so threadbare that all the pages came loose, I held them together with some rubber bands.

Mythology has never been out of print. I could easily have gotten myself a new copy any time. Instead, when it began to crumble and flake, making a bit of a mess on the shelf and even on the floor in front of the bookcase, I kept it in a plastic baggie. This did not look very attractive. But then it was not just a book: it was a memento of childhood, a holy thing.

One day about a year ago, while I was shopping for another book, a copy of Hamilton's *Mythology* caught my eye, and, thinking of my own pathetic copy back home, I decided the time had come finally to replace it. I bought the book and threw away the sandwich bag with its shabby remnants.

My new *Mythology* is also a mass-market paperback, the same size as the old one. It has a different, less striking cover, but the text is exactly the same, and it has the same Steele Savage drawings. In fact, page by page, the two editions are identical. What is lacking, though, is that irreplaceable thing: aura. I cannot look at the new book without feeling a pang.

I miss the old book, the blue and gold one, the one with the sexy cover. I want it back, that copy I read when most of life was ahead of rather than behind me—the one that accompanied me on that fierce, mysterious journey when a little-kid fascination with monsters like Medusa and the Chimaera gave way to infatuation with the bold and beautiful young men who killed them.

I want the same book that belonged to my mother, the one that she read before me, the pages she turned with her own hand.

I wonder: Did I ask her, when I went away, if I could have it, or did I just take it? I know that one of the main reasons I was drawn to the book in the first place was precisely because it was one of her favorites, something *she* loved. And I remember how so many of those stories about trapped or imperiled women— women awaiting heroes, women (like Perseus' own Andromeda) awaiting rescue—seemed to be about her, in the same way that books I would read later, novels like *Madame Bovary* and *Anna Karenina*, seemed to be about her: stories about women who were beautiful but unhappy, so like my mother, who spent much of her time yearning for a distant land and a different life and wondering why the gods had abandoned her.

I want it back, the book that had everything to do with my becoming a writer: it was those myths that would inspire my first attempts at poetry and fiction. And when I grew up I would write my mother's story, her unhappy, immigrant's story, and in that first novel of mine (though I confess I'd completely forgotten this) appears that very copy of Edith Hamilton's *Mythology*.

Throw it out? How could I have made such a mistake? I should have kept that book all my life. Or at least until it disintegrated. No, even then. It should have been allowed to rest on the shelf until it was nothing but a little heap of tiny grains: sand in an hourglass.

Another Country

CHRIS ABANI

A living history is sung by telling its melody.
Antonio Machado

The book cover is a dirty faded beige. Paperback. Well worn. The price on the top right-hand corner floating over the blue wash of the Brooklyn Bridge is inked out in black. In the top left-hand corner, in a small, squared-off box, the word *Dell* attempts to hold on. In big block red letters *JAMES BALDWIN* spills into the phrase in black lowercase, "His magnificent best-selling novel," before swelling back up to the title in black caps and the same size as Jimmy's name: *Another Country*. This weighty assertion of letters holds the left side of the cover grounded, the way I tell my students that the left side of a poem controls form. On the right side, the aforementioned Brooklyn Bridge is a blue-gray and seems to be growing out of a cluster of four people made for a Benetton ad. A black man's face sporting an Afro floats over a white woman's face also in the same blue-gray wash of the bridge. Directly below this couple is another interracial couple in flesh tones and full color, half-naked and clearly in ecstasy, positioned in proportion to the top like a careful math equation. A gold medallion announces: 2 ½ million copies sold!

This is my copy of James Baldwin's *Another Country*, inherited from my parents' bookcase in 1976.

My mother opened the world of books up to me. It was she who not only read to me when I was very young but also taught me to read by the time I was four. But there is something even greater than the gift of reading and that was the gift of uncensored reading.

I grew up in a very middle-class West African home with all of its usual access to privilege and the expectations that came with that, but even beyond that, for me, was the amount of intellectual privilege. My parents' bookcases were filled with all kinds of books—encyclopedias, *Reader's Digest*, the Koran, the Mahabharata in several volumes, nearly the entire catalog of Heinemann's African Writers Series, Agatha Christie, Somerset Maugham, Iris Murdoch, and on—and I was allowed, even encouraged, to read them at will, with my age being no barrier. By the time I was ten I had devoured *Crime and Punishment*, *The Brothers Karamazov*, the Koran, all the Robert Ludlum I could find, Agatha Christie, *Sherlock Holmes*, H. Rider Haggard, *Watership Down*, *The Jungle Book*, and the usual young boy's fare of comics—*The Silver Surfer*, *Batman*, etc.—the titles and authors as interchangeable as the concept of high- and lowbrow.

Then I came across a book shoved into the bookcase spine inward, ruffled earmarked pages fanning out. A rumple of white in a long line of hard and paperback spines, like a flower. I was curious because no one ever dared mistreat a book in my house. I sensed in a way that the freedom I had been granted to read all the other books, the same freedom that allowed me to sit in with the adults listening as they argued politics, literature, and religion—all of that seemed to have been halted at the book stuffed into the bookcase so I couldn't read the spine and would probably pass it by. Of course it was about me, wasn't everything?

Or perhaps my mother had stuffed it in this way fully expecting that I would pause at it, unable to pass it up. Either way, I pulled it out and tucked it in between the covers of my school reader. It was slim enough to hardly make a bulge. I would read it later when I could be uninterrupted. Perhaps after school in the cashew tree stuffing my face.

The book smells musty. It has for a long time and in spite of my repeated attempts to air it out, it continues to smell faintly of mildew. There is also a texture to it, to the cover and the pages, of age, of dirt even, accumulated through years of dusty tropical handling and periods of humid rest. It feels as though the book has contaminated my hands, as though the book left something of itself on me, and I immediately want to wash my hands to escape the world of it and return to this one.

    The first time I opened the book, it was two days after I had taken it off the shelf and rearranged *Robin Hood* to take its place, pages fanning out. I was lying on the back porch of the little Anglican chapel on the campus of McGregor Teacher Training College where my father was the principal. I got home from school early and, packing the book into my knapsack (I guess I'm dating myself here) along with some crackers and a soda, I headed out before anyone could ask where I was going. It was a cloudy day and rain was imminent, a fact that made me happy. When it rained it rained, thick blankets of water that seemed intent on reminding the ground who was in charge. Sodden—that's the word that comes to mind after a tropical rainfall. A rain like that could keep a person trapped somewhere for hours, the perfect alibi for reading something forbidden. Curled up on a bench just out of reach of the rain, I lost all sense of time. Soon the rain lulled me to sleep. I don't know how long I slept but I was awoken by a peal of thunder to find I had dropped the book and a slow trickle of water had pooled around it. Halfway through, where it had fallen, still open, there would grow a stain over the next few weeks. I shook it and spread it open like a bird on the back to dry while I waited for the rain to stop and wondered about New York and Rufus and the world of Baldwin.

About halfway through the book, and for nearly twenty pages, there is a mottled wash that spreads like fungi across the pages. Miraculously, none of the words are erased although there is some seepage of the ink; the pattern looks wonderful and reminds me of the pattern I once saw on a baobab tree as a child, caused, my elder brother told me, by the way water in the trunk would boil in the heat and release steam. An affliction that makes the tree more beautiful for it.

On the inside cover, there is a fragment of a Hafiz poem in green ink:

> *Even after all this time,*
> *the sun never says to the earth,*
> *"You owe me."*
> *Look what happens with a love like that.*
> *It lights the whole sky.*

This is from the time when I had attempted to give the book to a girl I thought I loved. I was sixteen, I was in love with words, I had told her what the book meant to me. She gently returned it and said: It's not even that you gave me a book instead of jewelry, but couldn't you even have bought me a new one?

The flyleaf of the book is turned out roughly and the wound of its loss is still visible in the book. That page had held my name written in my then somewhat childish scrawl and the publication date and other edition information. I often touch this part of the book to remind myself of the violence that words and books can and often do incite. I was an eleven-year-old when that particular wound was inflicted, a young seminarian, full of the desire to serve God and looking forward to a life of prayer, service, and meditation. One of the priests saw me reading, for the eighth time, *Another Country*. I didn't know at the time that Baldwin's books were banned in the seminary, nor did I fully understand the homosexuality he wrote about, and all the fuss that seemed to cause. I just knew that Jimmy wrote about love, and all of it was so irradiated by light as to be an actual glow off the pages.

I have come to realize over the years that the most sacred places are often the most private: churches, chapels, temples. It is as though people are afraid of the solitude of these places, perhaps of the truths they reveal about us. Anyway, I was sitting at the back of the chapel reading when a young priest happened upon me, as I said before. Seeing the book he pounced on it, but I wrested it from him and ran, leaving the page with my name firmly clutched in his fist. I never told them where I hid it, despite the punishment.

I published my first story at ten, a short morality tale called "The Lion," in the *State Newspaper*. It wasn't my first attempt to be a writer, but it was my first attempt with any serious intent, with any notion that what I was doing was no longer just play, just something I was good at. My first story, written at six, was a reinterpretation of the King Wenceslas story for homework, and my teacher, convinced that I had cheated, sent me home to an irate mother who drove me straight back to school to give the teacher a piece of her mind, a glorious day for me as I didn't like my teacher much. But "The Lion" was different because it was mine, an original, written with every intention of getting it published, with all the self-assured hubris that only a ten-year-old can muster. It was a story about a subject and a situation that I knew only from reading Kipling's work: A boy gives up his life to save his friends from a lion attack. I have never seen a lion outside of a zoo, and in the suburban neighborhood I grew up in, the only danger to a boy was having his pocket money stolen by the school bully.

All of my protagonists, then and since, have been marked by the existential melancholy of Dostoyevsky's Raskolnikov and Marvel Comics' Silver Surfer, but it was James Baldwin and *Another Country* that were the catalysts not only for my desire to become a writer but also for my imagination to take shape and conceptualize the possibilities. I wrote and published my first novel, *Masters of the Board*, at sixteen, and I believe that Baldwin's *Another Country*, more than any other book, was directly responsible for this and has also helped to shape over the years the core of my philosophical engagement with the world.

On page 72 there is a coffee stain—a dark ring with a few spots flecking the page around it, the spots like minor planets orbiting a gas giant.

When I moved to London in 1992, my sister and I shared an apartment and the incessant nighttime clatter of my old Royal and, later, Remington typewriters drove her crazy. All day I worked at the local welfare office, for the most part denying clients their claims for unemployment or chasing down lost checks for irate clients, and at night I would sit at my desk and pluck with two fingers at my typewriter, using so much Wite-Out that the finished pages were more like conceptual art than pages of a novel in progress. I would sit drinking cup after cup of coffee while Miles Davis played in the background. When I was stuck, which I often was, I would turn to *Another Country* for inspiration. Baldwin and an old illustrated Bible I had found in seminary never left my desk.

Above my desk in Los Angeles as I write this, deadline looming, is a picture of Baldwin—those familiar big eyes, that uncompromising piercing gaze, that face so ugly it can only really be called beautiful. He is my muse, has been for a while, and I collect every story I can about him and add them to my own, to my singular encounter with his novel as a ten-year-old.

In many ways I feel that as a thinker, he got to all the best ideas before me, and stripped them bare in language I can only envy, with a style and craft that I am still trying to emulate.

A lot has been written about *Another Country*, about how it fails as a novel. How its structure of three sections could be separate novels, that the parts do not hold up. There is much talk about it being an essay on America in novelistic form, as though this were a bad thing. But at its heart, just as with Salman Rushdie's *The Satanic Verses* and Don DeLillo's *The Body Artist*, *Another Country* is a writer's book, and Baldwin, a writer's writer. In this novel, Baldwin takes America to the operating table and flays its body open with a love so tender it burns, revealing all its hate, and shortcomings, beauty, pride, and flaws; this is something a young African understands well. How one can love and despise his nation at the same time, and how this ambiguity is perhaps a deeper patriotism than that easily announced from rooftops.

But *Another Country* is also a book about how to be a writer, filled with passages about this struggle, about how the weight of paper is a pressure sometimes too hard to bear, how the song of typewriters in stifling rooms is an aria, and how one can even begin to approach the sheer terror and unbearable harmony of this deep song.

I have also come to a startling (for me) realization about *Another Country*. The novel is not really about the many themes it tackles—homosexual love and prejudice, racism, misogyny, capitalism, fear, racialized sexual tension, suicide, and more. It is in fact an anthem to the transformative power of love; not an easy Hallmark-card sentiment but the twisted, tragic, and flawed love we find in *King Lear*. What James Baldwin seems to be arguing is that there is only one aberration in the world, the absence of love.

One of *Another Country*'s biggest achievements is precisely the fact that it doesn't hold together the way a more conventional novel does. It pushes not only the limits of the form but also the form's ability to mirror a kind of imagination that is wide and fractured as it attempts to push past the mundane to something deeper, something Baldwin loved to call *human*.

To write this essay, I reread *Another Country* perhaps for the twentieth time now, trying to keep the pages from falling apart. I have decided to buy another copy, to tide me over the next twenty years, but I cannot imagine this one being replaced by another paper copy, so I spent hours chasing down an electronic copy to download to my iPad.

I am unable, however, to find one—not on Google Books, or Project Gutenberg or even on Amazon's Kindle shop.

This makes me sad and extremely happy.

Heart's Needle

―――――――

CHRISTINE SCHUTT

W(illiam) D(e Witt) Snodgrass, born in Pennsylvania, 1926, died in New York, 2009. *Heart's Needle*, his first book, won the 1960 Pulitzer Prize in Poetry—and many other prizes besides. The title is from a narrative sequence of poems to his daughter. I read these particular poems on my bed in the summer on a "perfectly glorious"—my grandmother speaking—afternoon. I was reading on my belly with a pillow under my chin. The bedspread was a rusty-red print, English-quaint, Laura Ashley or Liberty, and the sun in the west-facing window was white, a great part of the room was as white as heaven, but where I was on my bed, the room was shady and cool. My feet—my toes— were cold and the pillow was . . . was there. Then I forgot myself and when I came to again I felt spoken to, tendered apologies, regrets sentimental and not, but deeply, deeply satisfying to hear.

Nature's cruelty sobers the poems; she is hardly maternal— windstorms and floods and "killdeers flying / all night over the mudflats crying" for nests lost—"starlings, dead." There is something dead in all the seasons Snodgrass recalls. From his daughter's birth, "when the new fallen soldiers froze / In Asia's steep ravines," to the last image in the sequence, father and daughter on a spring outing at the zoo:

If I loved you, they said, I'd leave
and find my own affairs.
Well, once again this April, we've
come around to the bears;

punished and cared for, behind bars,
the coons on bread and water
stretch thin black fingers after ours.
And you are still my daughter.

The image of animals behind bars, common creatures, famished on criminal fare, out of reach, precedes the father's emphatic assertion of paternal constancy and forecasts the greater hungers to be felt by both parent and child in the story of divorce—in the story of any family really, intact or otherwise.

At fifteen, I focused on otherwise, on difference, on absence whenever I was in the company of families. My grandmother was seventy-two years old when I moved in and made her home mine. (Mother was unwell and resting somewhere.) My grandmother had taken me in on other occasions and was glad to take me in for good; she was interested in whatever elixir might keep her young. She thought a teenager would help. And we lived well together and were happy; we shared a love of paper, pencils, pens, typewriters, and typing. My grandmother was an editor of a magazine called *Creative Wisconsin*, which featured stories and poems of a sweet cast and all to do with the Badger State. When it came to literature, her motto was simple: "I would rather smell the daisies than the shit." (History was an exception, of course, by which she meant American history, Indians, rural Wisconsin, and the disappearance of the passenger pigeon. She had been a girl and witness to that now extinct bird in its last few seasons when the skies were blackened by their passing. The title to the novel she could not bring herself to finish writing was *Passenger*

Pigeon.) I showed her "Daddy," by Sylvia Plath—another crush. "Why ever would I want to know this?" she asked. The poem was from an anthology an English teacher had lent me: *Contemporary American Poetry*, edited by Donald Hall, still in print. I think I did not share W. D. Snodgrass, whose poems, some from the *Heart's Needle* sequence, were also in this anthology, but maybe I did and maybe she said nothing—mute as ever on the subject of fathers. So it may be said my high school English teacher introduced me to Snodgrass. But the book itself?

How did I come to own *Heart's Needle*, this book so clearly mine? Nothing lent; jacketless, yes, but nothing faded about it, the same red on both sides. I think it was a serious gift from me to me. There is the bookplate with the spreading oak and under its roots my name, Christine Costigan.

Who was I then that I am not now?

I am not Christine Costigan, for one. My stepfather's surname is gone; I never liked it. A shared name does not confer consanguinity; a shared name does not keep families together: Why ever did Mother, who insisted on the adoption, believe it would? Sad, a handful of years were all we had as a family, then not a family, followed by a few aimless Sundays with Dad. One Sunday he telephoned to say he wasn't coming out to my grandmother's; in fact, he wasn't coming out to see me again, at all—ever. He declined my invitation to the father-daughter pancake-thing; he declined to be my father. "Because you never wrote me from camp, now, did you?" But I didn't have his new address! Where did he live? He lived in a kettle in a clover-leafed community of lean, like houses, mean windows, sparse lawns. My stepfather lived in a disappointment I never even saw. I made it up.

"You're a snob," my stepfather said, and I was. "You get that from your grandmother," he said. Maybe I did. I took my uncle to the father-daughter pancake breakfast and poured syrup over even the potatoes. No more Costigan. Jack Costigan—"Jackson" in his jazzy days or "Daddy-O"—a bit of a sleaze. Where is he now, I wonder? Still alive in diapers?

Fathers left, or mine did. Only W. D. Snodgrass was steadfast.

Robert Lowell, in a letter, describes Snodgrass as "green and hysterical personally and rather unhinged by ten days in New York." Lowell makes his costume out to be as goofy as his name: "plaid socks, wooly white underwearlike trousers, a coat made of white fibers and carbon and Ithaca New York tailoring." Merciless ridicule. Lowell claims Snodgrass spoke in a whisper and giggled.

Not true! At least not true of the man I saw or heard when I read *Heart's Needle*. No, the father speaking in Snodgrass's voice was my father, my real father, and so looked like him: slimly turned out, a lighthearted kind of handsome, crinkly eyes. His name was Maas. Jack Maas. Once people said we looked alike, and I have seen a resemblance in photographs of him, from his wedding, their wedding, in my grandmother's garden, a theatrical event, broadly recorded as society events were then—late 1940s. Photographs from that opulent union have appeared more than once in the state historical society's calendars, so I know my father's face well—knew it well enough to think I saw him once on a street in Chicago. This was not my city though it could have been his: anything is possible when nothing is known. I followed the man only as far as I dared. "Don't wander too far," my grandmother had said and I didn't. I stood against the slab that served as roof and cornice for his house.

My grandmother never spoke of him, and I never asked; whereas Mother told me things I didn't want to know. "We fucked like rabbits!" she said more than once.

"Don't tell me!" I shouted.

She said too much or nothing. A vacancy in a dust mote, overdrugged and noddy, Mother was scary, and I was glad to have gotten away and wanted to be in all ways away. I did not often visit.

Heart's Needle is taken from an old Irish story, *The Frenzy of Suibhne.* "An only daughter is the needle of the heart" is Suibhne's response to the news his daughter is dead. A daughter is the needle of the heart and to lose her, to suffer separation of any sort, is an astonishment of bright, brief pains, assaults repeated in the landscape. Regret was the sound I heard most when I first read these poems; I hear it still. The daughter is missed—how satisfying it was to know we were grieving together—and I fell into the father's address as into him. "Child of my winter, born" the sequence begins. The word *child* appears some ten times and always in melancholy context: "Child, we've done our best," says the father, resignedly referring to a late-April garden they have made; alas, when the garden blooms, he will be gone. *Heart's Needle* is reassurance of a father's remorse:

> *I get numb and go in*
> *though the dry ground will not hold*
> *the few dry swirls of snow*
> *and it must not be very cold.*
> *A friend asks how you've been*
> *and I don't know . . .*

In a family series of portrait photographs—black and white, lighted, different poses, pairings, us dressed up—is one that is most of my father to me. He is reading to me. I am in his lap but looking out at the photographer with a blurry, troublous expression. Something the photographer squeaked, the lights moved—brightened? Something has disturbed this twosome, and I am not quite two and my father is not quite forty-two. We are two against one, and who knows, maybe others, which might explain why I huddle in his lap, looking distrustful. But the redoubt of his posture is reassuring as is the kindly way he looks down— looks a little at me and not just at the book.

> *You bring back how the red-*
> *winged blackbird shrieked, slapping frail wings,*
>   *diving at my head—*
> *I saw where her tough nest, cradled, swings,*
>   *in tall reeds that must sway*
> *with the winds blowing every way.*
> *If you recall much, you recall this place.*

The lines tumble forward even in their backward gaze and are seductive. Hurrah for the power the daughter has to torment the father! "You raise into my head / a Fall night that I came once more / to sit on your bed." Remembering other seasons together, he agonizes, "You bring things I'd as soon forget." Here in the sixth poem of the sequence is a reenactment of what I wish had happened between my father and me—and, if I were honest, my stepfather and me—a scene of apology, an explanation, an acknowledgment of my predominance. Also, the pleasure—a tad sexual—in knowing that the father has suffered in his severance from his child. His first, I think. His daughter. Me.

> *Of all things, only we*
> *have power to choose that we should die;*
>   *nothing else is free*
> *in this world to refuse it. Yet I,*
>   *who say this, could not raise*
>   *myself from bed how many days*
> *to the thieving world. Child, I have another wife,*
>   *another child. We try to choose our life.*

My real father may still be alive. I was given a phone number not long ago; I lost it. Now the woman who said she was my father's sister is dead; the line is cut.

If I have learned anything this year, I have learned this much: like my fathers, I am stingy with love, and what I have written here is as close to an apology, a letter from camp, as I will ever write.

Ship of Fools

JONATHAN MILES

The entirety of my inheritance, when my mother dies, will be books. I've negotiated this with my two older sisters, who, between them, have laid gentle and awkward claim to the china, silver, jewelry, paintings, furniture, and other assorted heirlooms. Most of this—the books, the china, etc.—is presently housed inside a pair of climate-controlled storage units somewhere near Cleveland, while my mother, who, at seventy-five, is in the middle stages of Alzheimer's disease, lives in a nursing home, also near Cleveland, though sometimes she claims to be living in West Virginia, or New York, or Arizona. I suspect my sisters were relieved when I asked for the books, and only the books. We've watched other families splinter into bitter factions over tea sets and stamp collections and othersuch, and have vowed not to end up apportioning my mother's belongings in the manner of an acid divorce proceeding. My sisters are both a decade older than me, and partly because of that, but mostly due to the dissimilar circumstances of our raising (geographical, financial, psychological), they had different childhoods than I did. They're nostalgic about their youths—that nostalgia amplified by a genetic strain of Irish sentimentalism—whereas I spent years laboring, in distant isolation, to evict portions of mine from memory. And while I long ago abandoned the banal resentments of having suffered

an imperfect childhood, I have zero desire, nonetheless, to stock-
pile reminders of it.

With the exception of the books. There's not an extraordinary
amount of them: three hundred volumes, tops. And to deem
their value even *negligible* would be trumped-up flattery; were I
to sell the whole lot of them, at the Strand bookstore on Broadway, I'd be lucky to yield enough money for lunch for two, drinks
and tip excluded. A book collector, sifting through the boxes,
would probably characterize them, on the whole, as a typical
snapshot of the literary middlebrow of the 1960s, '70s, and '80s.
A sizable fraction probably came into the house via the mailman,
as Book-of-the-Month Club main selections: all the pop history,
with an emphasis on WWII (William Shirer, William Manches-
ter), the brand-name historical fiction (James Michener, Leon
Uris, Herman Wouk), and the vaguely leftist treatises (Irving
Howe) that didn't jibe with my parents' Eisenhower Republican-
ism. Those books aside, my imaginary collector might be able to
piece together a mental portrait of the lot's owner: a mother
(Erma Bombeck), a Catholic (Andrew C. Greeley), an Irish-
woman (Frank O'Connor, Maeve Binchy, "treasuries" of Irish
humor), an artist or at least an art appreciator (coffee-table books
about El Greco and Raphael and Rembrandt). But then he'd ar-
rive at the books resisting easy categorization, the ones he'd be
unable to snare in the net of stereotype, and those I consider her
library's true beating heart: the complete works, in some cases, of
Guy de Maupassant, Somerset Maugham, Ernest Hemingway,
Katherine Anne Porter, James Joyce, Gustave Flaubert. These
were the books my mother cherished, reread, and often tried
pressing onto her recalcitrant son, urging, *Read this, oh you must
read this.*

I think of all those books, lined neatly on shelves, religiously
dusted, as one of the primary landscapes of my early childhood.
I am afflicted with a ferociously leaky memory, unable to conjure

a single vision, for instance, of my elementary school, or, independent of photographs, the beloved grandfather I lost at age nine. With spooky accuracy, however, I can recall the title, author, and shelf placement of nearly all my mother's books. (My late father, I should note, read only newspapers. His sole contribution to the bookshelves was Edmund G. Love's *A History of the 7th Infantry Division in World War II*, which, being an account of his wartime experience, was in some small way my father's own biography—middle section of the bookcase, second row down, about five books in from the left.) For what must have been hours, I would sit staring at those books, dreamily, the way an infant ogles a crib mobile. Sometimes I'd pull one down, and try, unsuccessfully, to make sense of its contents. I remember an early attempt to read Porter's *Ship of Fools*, which had an appealing, breezy-sounding title (I pictured Noah's Ark, but with clowns in lieu of animals); I'm certain I never made it past the epigraph from Baudelaire, in its original French. But whatever questions I had about the world, those books, I felt sure, could answer—from what plump women looked like naked (Raphael's paintings cleared up that idle mystery) to what awful things had happened to my father on Okinawa to make him tighten his lips and wag his head silently whenever I or anyone else would ask him about it. I made the connection early: The things my mother knew—all her venerable, grownup knowledge of life and its workings—were derived from those shelves. Here was the mother lode.

By the time I was old enough to dig into those books, however, to follow my mother's path to knowledge and readerly joy the way I used to trail my father's bootprints through the deep, lake-effect snow, it was too late. We'd moved, disastrously, to Phoenix—economic refugees from the Rust Belt, who, like many others, experienced Sunbelt migration as an updating of Woody Guthrie's "Do Re Mi," as a wrecked and mangled fantasy.

Depression claimed my mother, then came for my father, too. He'd leave for months at a time, gone off to work somewhere, anywhere, while I'd sulk away my after-school hours alone in concrete drainage ditches, torturing scorpions with a stick. The new house smelled of ruin, soured dreams. Slamming doors marked our passages from room to room, trailed by the sniffly sounds of tears. The backyard swimming pool that had epito-mized our ambitions came to seem like a wretched blue joke; one night my father jumped in, fully dressed in a suit and tie, in what I suppose was an imitation of suicide, a practice run to see how a bridge jump might feel. Whatever my mother had gleaned from all her reading—from those endless, contented, Midwestern nights on the sofa, her face obscured behind a novel while, across the room on a chair, mine was similarly obscured behind a chil-dren's book—was clearly insufficient, a sham, an affectation: Just look where it had gotten us.

So I turned against books, or at least (because I was doomed, by nature, to be bookish) the books she approved. This was my earliest rebellion, predating adolescence: mild but not quite be-nign. I dove headfirst into horror novels, sci-fi, gruesome true-crime, Mickey Spillane potboilers, Gothic erotica—the kinds of books she disdained, *because* she disdained them. Much more rebellion would follow—my first arrest at thirteen, an appetite for death-metal, predictably long hair, gobs of cigarettes and drugs, a motorcycle, dropping out of high school and leaving home, permanently, at seventeen—but this is how it began: as a quiet rebuttal to her literary taste, a middle finger to the stan-dards she'd tried to instill. When I took up fishing, as an alterna-tive to the mopey lassitude of torturing scorpions, she suggested some of Hemingway's angling stories. I sneered. A few years later, while trying to decipher the meaning of the Ozzy Osbourne song "Mr. Crowley," a paean to the British occultist Aleister Crowley, I discovered *The Magician*, Somerset Maugham's novelization of Crowley's wicked, weird life. But Maugham, I knew, was one of my mother's idols. Sigh. Without reading *The Magician*, I abandoned the deciphering project and Ozzy along with it. Obviously something harder was called for.

But that was then. Now I am slipping toward forty, with three children of my own, and she, God help her, is adrift in a mental open sea, surrounded by the bobbing debris of her memories, clinging to whatever slippery remnants she can. One of the many dismal effects of Alzheimer's disease is that it not only erases memory but warps it, so that old memories are constantly re-filed as new, rendering the present indistinguishable from the past. In her mind, my father dies, returns from the dead, dies again, returns again bearing flowers. I am eleven years old, then a married father of three, then a twentysomething, aspiring *artiste* in Mississippi, then eleven years old again, with her panicking because I'm not home from school. Reality is no match to the vividness of these miscataloged memories. How is it possible, she wonders aloud, for my father to so effortlessly shuttle back and forth between life and death? She admits the absurdity of this, but not the unreality of it. Yet I'm aware that one day, not far in the future, I may look back at these moments with something like nostalgia—when that morning comes, as it does for many Alzheimer's patients, when she does not recognize me at all, when I am no longer eleven or nearing forty or anywhere in between, when the disease has vanquished me altogether, and my sisters and children with me—when the last of the debris has sunk into that sea, and she floats alone in a featureless gray expanse.

I have before me, as I write this, her copy of *Ship of Fools*, which I swiped from her apartment after my father died in 2007, and finally read, with awe and gratitude, just a few months ago. It's the hardback edition, from 1962. The dust jacket is missing, so there is only Porter's signature on the ginger-colored cover.

Inside the book, on the title page, is my mother's signature, in an idiosyncratic cursive modeled precisely upon her mother's. Though it has been sitting here on my desk in my cigarette-clouded office for weeks, the book still smells, when I press my nose against it, of my mother's perfume, and of a certain lost era, perhaps: the kinetic, overlit past as glimpsed in 8 mm home movies, those prelapsarian days of fat, shaky-legged toddlers and epic snow forts and neighborhood block parties, of cousins and grandparents flitting into the camera frame, of shiny new sedans and regular employment, back before everything curdled in the desert heat.

I was nine years from being born when Porter published *Ship of Fools*, but I can imagine how it entered our house (inside a shopping bag from the Halle Bros. department store in downtown Cleveland) and how my mother must have gobbled up its pages. Porter's masterwork was two decades in the making; for years, Harcourt Brace would announce its publication date, then retract it, as Porter kept tinkering and retinkering with the novel. Already a fan of Porter's short stories, my mother must have been monitoring the book's protracted gestation with impatient eagerness, though she would have read it, I suspect, even without the personal interest. She was always a devoted reader of book reviews—and remains so, even today—and has always been vulnerable to hype. The publication of *Ship of Fools*, so long overdue, was a cultural *event* back in '62, in the way a new HBO series from David Simon or a product from Apple reaps saturation media coverage nowadays. Craving hipness, my mother would have been unable to resist it. She was the kind of reader Philip Roth once lamented as an endangered species: "people who . . . think that, after dinner tonight, and after the kids are in bed, I'm going to read for two hours," and who, while they read, "don't watch television or answer the phone." Not an intellectual, by most measures—with Joyce, for example, my mother adored

Dubliners and *Portrait of the Artist as a Young Man*, but her affection stopped short of *Ulysses* and *Finnegan's Wake*. Instead, she was an average citizen—an Ohio housewife, a maker of pies and casseroles—who considered it her pleasurable duty to stay abreast of literary culture, whose surveillance of the ever-shifting world she accomplished via books.

Books like Porter's. *Ship of Fools* is an allegorical novel—a fat, unwieldy, and intermittently satirical depiction of a transatlantic sea voyage in 1931, when Nazism was starting its creep through Germany. Its characters—and there are dozens of them, minutely drawn, and woven into a dense panoply of subplots—are constantly bumping into latent evil (mostly in the guise of anti-Semitism, though a precious little dog gets tossed overboard also) and either retreating from it or submitting to it, in much the way Europe responded to Nazism, until it was too late. They're all too preoccupied, in one way or another, with "pulling a geographical," as they say in Alcoholics Anonymous—trying to change their lives by changing their latitude, fleeing toward some utopian place where "all shall be well," to crib from Julian of Norwich, "and all manner of things shall be well." I wonder, if my mother were to reread it now, whether she would note the thematic parallels to her own history, to the ruinous geographical she and my father pulled when they packed up the Oldsmobile and replanted us in Phoenix, dizzied by visions of a western utopia brimming with sunlight and easy wealth. Probably not. Even before the Alzheimer's began expunging her memory, she had a knack for creative remembrance, for repainting the past with her own, more brightly hued palette.

It's an abstract thought, however. She cannot reread it, in her present and future state, not to mention that I've claimed her copy of the novel (which has, for the moment, apparently dropped out of print). Her nightstand at the nursing home is still stacked with novels, but I can only imagine what reading must be for her now: an old habit, like praying the rosary, that's become more physical than mental. The words, the sentences, the scenes pass through her mind like fluids, leaving no residue. How terrible it must be to crack open a novel at the bookmark and have, at best, only a foggy memory of what's come before, and probably no recollection at all. The dim recognition of a character's name, perhaps. A vague sense of setting, if only at the continental level. Not long ago, during a visit, I found her reading Michael Dorris's *A Yellow Raft in Blue Water*. When I asked her what the novel was about, she frowned, and a long pained silence swamped the room. Then she turned to the back cover, and read aloud, in its entirety, the jacket copy. "So there," she said quietly. "That's what it's about."

Ship of Fools, with its thirty-eight named characters, would overwhelm her today. It would float through her mind like one of those wartime passenger liners, slipping across the inky sea with its lights off and its voices hushed, leaving no trace of itself save the fleeting, moon-colored froth of its wake. Yet her eyes glow when I mention that I've just read it. "Oh, isn't it wonderful?" she says, and I answer yes, yes it is. This provokes memories of her other favorites, and for a moment she brightens, stricken with a rare and welcome clarity. "Does anyone still read Hemingway?" she asks me, and I say yes, which pleases her, as if someone had complimented an old dress of hers as fashionable. It's how we make amends, she and I, for all the screaming fights and the grudges and resentments from decades ago, for all the psychic bruises we inflicted upon one another, for all the dumb misery that drove me from home as a confused teenager. Or at least it's how I make amends, since she has forgotten all the bruises—her memory loss, in this case, a balmy, pastel comfort. This is our neutral ground, and my inheritance: the physical books themselves, permanently infused with the scent of her perfume, as well as the hereditary desire to read them, to use books as a periscope for surveying the world, to confront life on the page. "What about Guy de Maupassant?" she asks, which forces me to confess I've yet to read him. She launches into an enthusiastic homage to de Maupassant, with surprisingly crisp recollection of certain stories, and instructs me to borrow her copy of his collected stories, which she fails to remember is packed away in a storage unit. I promise her I'll get to him someday— though if I'm reading her copy, I realize, feeling something sink inside of me, that someday will have come too late. "Oh, and Katherine Anne Porter," she says suddenly, rapturously. "Have you read her?" Yes, I say, *Ship of Fools*. "Isn't it wonderful?" she says, and I say yes, Mother, yes it is.

CONTRIBUTORS' NOTES

Chris Abani's prose includes *Song for Night* (Akashic, 2007), *The Virgin of Flames* (Penguin, 2007), *Becoming Abigail* (Akashic, 2006), *GraceLand* (FSG, 2004), and *Masters of the Board* (Delta, 1985). His poetry collections are *Sanctificum* (Copper Canyon Press, 2010), *There Are No Names for Red* (Red Hen Press, 2010), *Feed Me the Sun-Collected Long Poems* (Peepal Tree Press, 2010), *Hands Washing Water* (Copper Canyon, 2006), *Dog Woman* (Red Hen, 2004), *Daphne's Lot* (Red Hen, 2003), and *Kalakuta Republic* (Saqi, 2001). He holds a BA in English (Nigeria), an MA in Gender and Culture (Birkbeck College, University of London), and an MA in English and a PhD in Literature and Creative Writing (University of Southern California). He is a professor at the University of California–Riverside and the recipient of the PEN USA Freedom-to-Write Award, the Prince Claus Award, a Lannan Literary Fellowship, a California Book Award, a Hurston/Wright Legacy Award, a PEN Beyond the Margins Award, the PEN/Hemingway Award, and a Guggenheim Fellowship.

Rabih Alameddine is a painter and author. He was born in Amman, Jordan, and grew up in Kuwait and Lebanon. He was educated in England and America, and now divides his time between San Francisco and Beirut. Alameddine has had solo gallery shows in cities throughout the United States, Europe, and the Middle East. His previous books include *Koolaids: The Art of War* (1998), *The Perv* (1999), and *I, the Divine: A Novel in First Chapters* (2001). Alameddine received a Guggenheim Fellowship in 2002. His latest novel, *The Hakawati*, was published by Alfred A. Knopf in May 2008 and was an international bestseller. It will be published in fifteen countries. He is currently working on a novel tentatively titled *At the Quiet Limit of the World*.

Ray Bradbury is the author of more than three dozen books, including *Fahrenheit 451*, *The Martian Chronicles*, *Dandelion Wine*, and *Something Wicked This Way Comes*. He has written for the theater and cinema, including the screenplay for John Huston's classic adaptation of *Moby Dick*. He was nominated for an Academy Award, won an Emmy for his teleplay of *The Halloween Tree*, adapted sixty-five of his stories for television's *The Ray Bradbury Theater*, and received the National Medal of Arts in 2004. He lives in Los Angeles.

Anthony Doerr is the author of four books: *Memory Wall*, *The Shell Collector*, *About Grace*, and *Four Seasons in Rome*. Doerr's fiction has won three O. Henry Prizes and has been anthologized in *The Best American Short Stories*, *The Anchor Book of New American Short Stories*, and *The Scribner Anthology of Contemporary Fiction*. His work has been translated into eleven languages and has won awards including the Rome Prize, the New York Public Library's Young Lions Award, the Barnes & Noble Discover Prize, and the Ohioana Book Award twice. He lives in Boise, Idaho, with his wife and two sons.

Louis Ferrante made his reputation on the streets of New York as leader of his own crew of hijackers for the infamous Gambino Crime Family. The law eventually caught up with him and he spent eight and a half years in some of America's worst penitentiaries, where he read his first book and taught himself the art of writing. His memoir *Unlocked: The Life and Crimes of a Mafia Insider* was published by HarperCollins in 2009.

Nick Flynn is the author of two collections of poetry, a play, and the memoir *Another Bullshit Night in Suck City*, which won the PEN/Martha Albrand Award and was shortlisted for France's Prix Femina. His most recent book is *The Ticking Is the Bomb*. His poems, essays, and nonfiction have appeared in the *New Yorker*, *The Paris Review*, National Public Radio's *This American Life*, and the *New York Times Book Review*.

Karen Joy Fowler is the author of five novels and two short story collections. Her first novel, *Sarah Canary*, won the Commonwealth medal for best first novel by a Californian; her third, *Sister Noon*, was a finalist for the PEN/Faulkner Award; and *The Jane Austen Book Club* was a *New York Times* bestseller. She has won the Nebula Award twice for short fiction, and a new story collection is scheduled for fall 2010 from Small Beer Press. She currently lives in Santa Cruz, California, with her husband.

Julia Glass is the author of the novels *Three Junes*, winner of a National Book Award; *The Whole World Over*; and *The Widower's Tale*. Her third book, *I See You Everywhere*, a collection of linked stories, won the 2009 SUNY John Gardner Fiction Award. She has also won fellowships from the National Endowment for the Arts, the New York Foundation for the Arts, and the Radcliffe Institute for Advanced Study. Other awards for her fiction include the Sense of Place Award, the Tobias Wolff Award, and the Pirate's Alley Medal for Best Novella. Her essays have been widely anthologized. Julia lives with her two sons and their father in Massachusetts.

Karen Green is a visual artist.

David Hajdu is the music critic for *The New Republic* and a professor at the Columbia University Graduate School of Journalism. He is the author of four books, including *Heroes and Villains*, a collection of his essays.

Terrence Holt teaches in the Department of Social Medicine and practices in the Division of Geriatric Medicine at the University of North Carolina–Chapel Hill. A contributing editor at *Men's Health*, he has also written essays on medical practice for *Boston Review, Granta, Tin House,* and *The New Republic*. A collection of his short fiction, *In the Valley of the Kings*, was published last fall by W. W. Norton. He is currently at work on a collection of stories about medical training, titled *Internal Medicine*.

Sara Khalili is an editor and translator of contemporary Iranian literature. Her most recent translations include various short stories by Shahriar Mandanipour as well as his novel *Censoring an Iranian Love Story*. She is a recipient of the 2007 PEN Literary Award for Translation.

Jim Knipfel was a longtime columnist and staff writer at *New York Press*. He is the author of several books, including *Slackjaw, Unplugging Philco,* and *These Children Who Come at You with Knives*. He lives in Brooklyn.

Shahriar Mandanipour is regarded as one of the most successful contemporary writers in Iran. He has won numerous awards for his novels, short stories, and nonfiction, although he was unable to publish there from 1992 until 1997 as a result of censorship. His first novel to appear in English, *Censoring an Iranian Love Story*, was published by Knopf in 2009. He currently lives and works in Cambridge, Massachusetts.

Sarah Manguso is the author of four books, most recently the memoir *The Two Kinds of Decay*, which was published in five countries. She lives in Los Angeles.

Sean Manning is the author of *The Things That Need Doing: A Memoir* and editor of the nonfiction anthologies *Top of the Order, The Show I'll Never Forget,* and *Rock and Roll Cage Match*. He lives in New York.

Joyce Maynard (www.joycemaynard.com) is the author of four non-fiction books and seven novels—the most recent of which, *The Good Daughters*, was published in September 2010. Her bestselling memoir, *At Home in the World*, has been translated into eleven languages.

Philipp Meyer grew up in Baltimore, dropped out of high school when he was sixteen, and got a GED. After six years working as a bike mechanic and volunteering at a trauma center, he ended up at Cornell University. Upon graduation from Cornell he held a job as derivatives trader, followed by stints as a construction worker and ambulance driver. His first novel, *American Rust*, is being published in sixteen countries and ten languages. It was an *Economist* Book of the Year, a *Washington Post* Best Book of 2009, a *New York Times* Notable Book, and one of *Newsweek* magazine's "Best. Books. Ever.," in addition to making numerous other best-of-2009 lists. Meyer's other writing has been published in the *New York Times Book Review*, *The Guardian*, *The Independent*, *Esquire UK*, *McSweeney's*, *The Iowa Review*, *New Stories from the South*, and *Salon*. In 2008, he graduated from the Michener Center for Writers. In 2010, he received a Guggenheim Fellowship. He lives in Austin, Texas.

Jonathan Miles is the author of a novel, *Dear American Airlines*, which was named a *New York Times* Notable Book and was a finalist for the QPB New Voices Award, the Borders Original Voices Award, and the Great Lakes Book Award. His second novel, *Want Not*, will be published by Houghton Mifflin Harcourt. A former columnist for the *New York Times*, he lives in New York.

Sigrid Nunez is the author of six novels, including *The Last of Her Kind* and, most recently, *Salvation City*. Her memoir about Susan Sontag, *Sempre Susan*, will be published in spring 2011.

Ed Park is the author of the novel *Personal Days*, which was a finalist for the PEN/Hemingway Award. He is a founding editor of *The Believer*.

Victoria Patterson is the author of *Drift*, which was a finalist for the California Book Award and the 2009 Story Prize. Her work has appeared in various publications and journals, including the *Los Angeles Times*, *Orange Coast Magazine*, and *The Southern Review*. Her novel *This Vacant Paradise* is forthcoming from Counterpoint Press in February 2011. She lives with her family in Southern California and teaches through the UCLA Extension Writers' Program and as a lecturer at UC Riverside.

Francine Prose is a novelist and critic whose latest book, *Anne Frank: The Book, The Life, The Afterlife*, was published by Harper in October 2009. Her most recent novel, *Goldengrove*, was published by Harper-Collins in September 2008, and came out in paperback from Harper Perennial in September 2009. Her previous books include the novels *A Changed Man* and *Blue Angel*, which was a finalist for the 2001 National Book Award, and the nonfiction *New York Times* bestseller *Reading Like a Writer: A Guide for People Who Love Books and for Those Who Want to Write Them*. Her articles and essays have appeared in the *New Yorker*, *Harper's*, *The Atlantic*, *Condé Nast Traveler*, *ArtNews*, *Parkett*, *Modern Painters*, and the *New York Times Magazine*. She is the recipient of numerous grants and awards, among them the Dayton Literary Peace Prize, the Edith Wharton Achievement Award for Literature, and Guggenheim and Fulbright fellowships, and is a past president of PEN American Center. She lives in New York City.

Michael Ruhlman is a freelance journalist and writer as well as the author of nine nonfiction books and co-author of seven cookbooks, with two more scheduled for fall 2011. His most recent book is *Ratio: The Secret Codes Behind the Craft of Everyday Cooking*. His work has appeared in the *New York Times*, the *Los Angeles Times*, *Gourmet*, *Saveur*, and *Food Arts*, and has received International Association of Culinary Professionals (IACP) awards and a James Beard Award. He lives in Cleveland Heights, Ohio, with his wife and two children.

Elissa Schappell is the author of both *Use Me*, a finalist for the PEN/Hemingway Award, and of the forthcoming *Blueprints for Building Better Girls*. She is co-editor with Jenny Offill of the anthologies *The Friend Who Got Away* and *Money Changes Everything*. Her work has appeared in *The Paris Review*, *Spin*, *Bomb*, *The Mrs. Dalloway Reader*, *The Bitch in the House*, and *The KGB Bar Reader*. She is a contributing editor at *Vanity Fair* as well as a co-founder and now editor-at-large of *Tin House* magazine.

Christine Schutt is the author of two short story collections, *Nightwork* and *A Day, a Night, Another Day, Summer*. Her first novel, *Florida*, was a National Book Award finalist; her second novel, *All Souls*, a finalist for the 2009 Pulitzer Prize. Among other honors, Schutt has twice won the O. Henry Short Story Prize as well as Pushcart and *Mississippi Review* fiction prizes. She is the recipient of New York Foundation for the Arts and Guggenheim fellowships. Schutt lives and teaches in New York.

Jim Shepard is the author of six novels, most recently *Project X* (Knopf, 2004), and three story collections, including *Like You'd Understand, Anyway* (Knopf, 2007), which was nominated for the National Book Award and won the Story Prize.

Susan Straight has published six novels, including *Highwire Moon*, a finalist for the National Book Award, and *A Million Nightingales*. Her new novel *Take One Candle Light a Room* will be published in fall 2010 by Pantheon. She was born in Riverside, California, where she still lives with her family. Her essays and short stories have been published in *Harper's*, the *New York Times*, *Salon*, *The Nation*, and elsewhere.

J. Courtney Sullivan is the author of the bestselling novel *Commencement* (Knopf) and co-editor of the essay anthology *Click: The Moments That Made Us Feminists* (Seal Press). Her work has appeared in the *New York Times*, *New York*, *Elle*, *Glamour*, *Cosmopolitan*, *Allure*, *In Style*, *Men's Vogue*, the *New York Observer*, and *Tango*. Her novel *Maine* will be published by Knopf in May 2011. Find out more about Courtney at www.jcourtneysullivan.com.

Anthony Swofford is the author of the novel *Exit A* and the memoir *Jarhead*. He has taught at the University of Iowa Writers' Workshop, Lewis and Clark College, and elsewhere.

Danielle Trussoni is the author of *Falling Through the Earth: A Memoir*, which was chosen by the *New York Times* as one of the 10 Best Books of the Year in 2006. Her novel, the international bestseller *Angelology*, is being released in thirty-two countries. She currently lives in the south of France with her husband, the writer Nikolai Grozni, and their children.

Joanne Wang was born and raised in Beijing, China, and attended Fudan University in Shanghai, where she majored in English literature. She is a translator, interpreter, and literary agent with a strong focus on Chinese works. She lives in New York.

Xu Xiaobin was born in 1953 in Beijing, China. She spent nine years in the countryside and a factory during the Cultural Revolution (1966–1976). She graduated from the Central Institute of Finance and Banking and began publishing her writings in 1981. Currently she is a staff screenplay writer at China Central Television. In China, she has published five novels, twelve novellas, and ten collections of essays and prose. She lives in Beijing.

CONTRIBUTORS' CREDITS

"Foreword" copyright © 2010 by Ray Bradbury
"Introduction" copyright © 2010 by Sean Manning
"The Crying of Lot 49 and In the Heart of the Heart of the Country" copyright © 2010 by Jim Shepard
"Andersen's Fairy Tales" copyright © 2010 by Francine Prose
"The Stranger" copyright © 2010 by Anthony Swofford
"Speak, Memory" copyright © 2010 by Danielle Trussoni
"The Shadow of the Sun" copyright © 2010 by Nick Flynn
"The Bible" copyright © 2010 by Joyce Maynard
"Les Misérables" copyright © 2010 by Louis Ferrante
"Naked Lunch" copyright © 2010 by Elissa Schappell
"The Story and Its Writer" copyright © 2010 by Anthony Doerr
"Invisible Man" copyright © 2010 by David Hajdu
"Roar and More" copyright © 2010 by Julia Glass. Used with permission of Brandt & Hochman Literary Agents, Inc.
"Das Kapital" copyright © 2010 by Shahriar Mandanipour
"The Viking Portable Dorothy Parker" copyright © 2010 by J. Courtney Sullivan
"The Merck Manual of Diagnosis and Therapy, Eighth Edition" copyright © 2010 by Terrence Holt
"For Whom the Bell Tolls" copyright © 2010 by Philipp Meyer
"The Collected Stories of Amy Hempel" copyright © 2010 by Karen Green
"Mason & Dixon" copyright © 2010 by Jim Knipfel
"Emily Dickinson (Literature and Life)" copyright © 2010 by Xu Xiaobin
"Dungeon Masters Guide" copyright © 2010 by Ed Park
"Sula" copyright © 2010 by Susan Straight
"Ulysses" copyright © 2010 by Sean Manning

ACKNOWLEDGMENTS

For their help and encouragement, the editor thanks Jim Fitzgerald; Jonathan Crowe, John Radziewicz, Lissa Warren, Annie Lenth, Christine Arden, and everyone involved at Da Capo Press and the Perseus Books Group; Vanessa White Wolf; James Manning; and Susan Manning.